OpenGL to WebGL: Bridging the Graphics Divide

Kameron Hussain and Frahaan Hussain

Published by Sonar Publishing, 2023.

OPENGL TO WEBGL: BRIDGING THE GRAPHICS DIVIDE

First edition. November 27, 2023.

ISBN: 979-8223496045

Written by Kameron Hussain and Frahaan Hussain.

Table of Contents

3. Use Display Lists (Legacy OpenGL)

4. Texture Compression

5. Level of Detail (LOD)

6. Cull Backfaces

7. Batch Rendering

8. Asynchronous Loading

9. Shader Optimization

10. Memory Management

Section 9.3: Optimizing WebGL for Performance

1. Use RequestAnimationFrame

2. Minimize WebGL Context Loss

3. Batch WebGL Draw Calls

4. Use Efficient Data Formats

5. Texture Atlases and Texture Compression

6. Mipmap Levels

7. Shader Compilation and Linking

8. Avoid Synchronous Operations

9. Use Transform Feedback (if applicable)

10. Profile and Debug

11. WebGL Extensions

12. Reduce Overdraw

Section 9.4: Cross-Platform Optimization Techniques

1. Device Detection

2. Fallbacks and Progressive Enhancement

3. Resolution and Quality Levels

4. Adaptive Rendering

5. Responsive Design

6. Testing Across Platforms

7. Platform-Specific Optimization

8. WebGL Extensions and Fallbacks

9. Cross-Browser Compatibility

10. User Feedback

11. Continuous Optimization

Section 9.5: Debugging and Profiling Graphics Applications

1. Browser Developer Tools

2. WebGL Inspector

3. OpenGL Debugging Tools

4. Profiling Tools

5. Shader Debugging

6. Frame Capture and Analysis

1. Choosing a Project

2. Exploring Documentation and Issue Tracker

3. Forking the Repository

4. Cloning the Repository

Section 18.3: Leveraging Community Knowledge and Resources

1. Online Forums and Discussion Boards

2. Social Media and Networking

3. GitHub and Source Code Repositories

4. Online Courses and Tutorials

5. Graphics Conferences and Meetups

6. Reading Books and Documentation

7. Online Courses and Tutorials

8. Graphics Conferences and Meetups

9. Reading Books and Documentation

10. Collaboration and Contributions

11. Stay Informed

Section 18.4: Case Studies: Successful Community Projects

1. Three.js: A Popular WebGL Framework

2. GLM: The OpenGL Mathematics Library

8. WebGL in Web Development

9. Graphics APIs

10. Open Source Communities

Section 19.2: Emerging Technologies in WebGL and OpenGL

1. WebGPU: The Next-Generation Graphics API

2. Vulkan for the Web

3. WebAssembly (Wasm) Enhancements

4. Real-Time Collaboration in 3D Environments

5. AI-Driven Content Generation

6. Augmented Reality (AR) for the Web

7. 3D Web Design Tools

8. Continued VR/AR Integration

9. Cross-Platform Deployment

10. WebXR: Expanding Immersive Experiences

Section 19.3: The Future of Integrated Graphics Environments

1. Unified Graphics Ecosystem

2. Improved Realism and Immersion

3. Enhanced Performance and Optimization

4. Ray Tracing Integration

5. Cross-Device and Cross-Reality Experiences

6. Web3D and the Metaverse

7. Machine Learning and Procedural Content

8. WebGPU Adoption

9. Accessibility and Inclusivity

10. Sustainability and Efficiency

Section 19.4: Predictions and Speculations

1. Convergence of WebGL and OpenGL

2. WebAssembly and Native Performance

3. Integration with WebXR

4. Continued Emphasis on Security

5. AI-Driven Graphics

6. Environmental Considerations

7. Cross-Platform Accessibility

8. Quantum Computing Impact

9. Decentralized Graphics and NFTs

10. Ethical Considerations

Section 19.5: Preparing for Future Developments in Graphics Programming

1. Lifelong Learning

2. Embrace Cross-Disciplinary Skills

5. Diversify Your Skills

6. Ethical Considerations

7. Stay Passionate

Section 20.3: Future Pathways in Graphics Programming

1. Real-Time Ray Tracing

2. Machine Learning and Graphics

3. WebGL and WebXR Integration

4. Global Illumination

5. Cross-Platform Development

6. Ethics and Responsible AI

Section 20.4: Resources for Continued Learning

1. Online Courses and Tutorials

2. Books and Documentation

3. Community Forums and Blogs

4. GitHub and Open Source Projects

5. YouTube and Video Tutorials

6. Hackathons and Competitions

7. University Courses and Degrees

8. Professional Organizations and Conferences

9. Industry Journals and Publications

10. Networking and Collaboration

Section 20.5: Final Thoughts and Encouragement for Aspiring Developers

1. Celebrate Your Progress

2. Embrace Challenges

3. Keep Experimenting

4. Stay Curious

5. Collaborate and Share

6. Set Goals and Keep Learning

7. Adapt to Industry Trends

8. Maintain a Work-Life Balance

Chapter 1: Introduction to Graphics Programming

Section 1.1: The Evolution of Graphics Programming

Graphics programming has a rich history that has evolved significantly over the years. In this section, we'll delve into the fascinating journey of graphics programming, tracing its development from its early beginnings to the sophisticated technology it is today.

Early Beginnings

Graphics programming can trace its roots back to the early days of computing. In the mid-20th century, computers were rudimentary and lacked the graphical capabilities we take for granted today. Instead, they primarily focused on text-based output and data processing.

One of the earliest instances of computer-generated graphics can be found in the work of Ivan Sutherland, who developed the "Sketchpad" program in the early 1960s at MIT. This revolutionary program allowed users to interactively draw and manipulate shapes on a screen using a light pen, paving the way for future graphics innovations.

The Emergence of Computer Graphics

As computing power grew, so did the possibilities for graphics programming. In the 1970s and 1980s, computer graphics began to find applications in various fields, including engineering, entertainment, and scientific visualization. Researchers and engineers developed graphics hardware and software to create more sophisticated images and animations.

Birth of OpenGL

In the early 1990s, OpenGL (Open Graphics Library) emerged as a powerful graphics API (Application Programming Interface). Developed by Silicon Graphics Inc. (SGI), OpenGL was designed to provide a standardized way of interacting with graphics hardware. It quickly gained popularity among developers and became a fundamental technology for creating 2D and 3D graphics.

```
#include <GL/gl.h>

#include <GL/glut.h>

void display() {

// OpenGL rendering code here

// ...

glutSwapBuffers();

}

int main(int argc, char** argv) {

glutInit(&argc, argv);

glutInitDisplayMode(GLUT_DOUBLE | GLUT_RGB);

glutInitWindowSize(800, 600);

glutCreateWindow("OpenGL Example");

glutDisplayFunc(display);
```

```
glutMainLoop();

return 0;

}
```

Rise of WebGL

With the advent of the internet and web browsers, a new need arose – the ability to render graphics directly in web pages. This led to the development of WebGL, a JavaScript API based on OpenGL ES (Embedded Systems). WebGL brought the power of hardware-accelerated graphics to web applications, opening up new possibilities for web-based interactive graphics.

WebGL Example:

```
const canvas = document.getElementById("myCanvas");

const gl = canvas.getContext("webgl");

if (!gl) {

console.error("WebGL not supported, falling back on experimental-webgl");

gl = canvas.getContext("experimental-webgl");

}

if (!gl) {

alert("Your browser does not support WebGL");

}

// WebGL rendering code here
```

// ...

Conclusion

The evolution of graphics programming has been a journey from simple text-based displays to complex 3D rendering in real-time applications. This progression has been driven by advances in hardware, software, and the changing needs of various industries. In the chapters to come, we will explore the intricacies of graphics programming, both in the traditional OpenGL realm and the web-centric world of WebGL. We will delve into the core concepts, techniques, and best practices that will enable you to create stunning graphics and visualizations.

Stay tuned as we embark on this exciting journey through the world of graphics programming!

Section 1.2: Overview of OpenGL: History and Applications

OpenGL, or Open Graphics Library, has played a pivotal role in the development of graphics programming. In this section, we'll explore the history of OpenGL and its wide-ranging applications in various domains.

History of OpenGL

OpenGL was first developed by Silicon Graphics Inc. (SGI) in the early 1990s. It was created as an open, platform-independent API for rendering 2D and 3D graphics. SGI aimed to provide a standardized way for developers to interact with graphics hardware, allowing for greater portability of applications across different platforms.

OpenGL quickly gained popularity due to its versatility and performance. It became the foundation for graphics development across industries such as gaming, computer-aided design (CAD), scientific visualization, and more. Over the years, OpenGL has undergone several updates and revisions, with each version introducing new features and capabilities.

Key Features of OpenGL

One of the key strengths of OpenGL is its ability to harness the power of hardware acceleration. It allows developers to take full advantage of the graphics processing unit (GPU) for rendering, resulting in high-performance graphics. OpenGL also provides a consistent and flexible programming model, enabling developers to create complex 2D and 3D graphics with ease.

OpenGL's architecture is based on a state machine model, where various states and parameters can be set to control rendering. This model provides fine-grained control over the rendering process, allowing developers to achieve the desired visual effects.

```
// Example OpenGL code to draw a simple triangle

#include <GL/gl.h>

#include <GL/glut.h>

void display() {

glClear(GL_COLOR_BUFFER_BIT);

glBegin(GL_TRIANGLES);

glVertex2f(-0.5f, -0.5f);

glVertex2f(0.5f, -0.5f);
```

```
glVertex2f(0.0f, 0.5f);
glEnd();
glFlush();
}
int main(int argc, char** argv) {
glutInit(&argc, argv);
glutInitDisplayMode(GLUT_SINGLE | GLUT_RGB);
glutInitWindowSize(800, 600);
glutCreateWindow("OpenGL Example");
glutDisplayFunc(display);
glutMainLoop();
return 0;
}
```

Applications of OpenGL

OpenGL has found applications in a wide range of fields, making it a versatile and widely adopted graphics API. Here are some notable areas where OpenGL has made a significant impact:

1. Gaming

OpenGL has been a cornerstone of the gaming industry, providing the graphics rendering capabilities needed for immersive 3D games.

Many popular games have utilized OpenGL for rendering realistic environments and characters.

2. CAD and 3D Modeling

In the field of computer-aided design (CAD) and 3D modeling, OpenGL is extensively used to create and manipulate complex 3D models. Engineers and designers rely on OpenGL to visualize and simulate their designs.

3. Scientific Visualization

Scientific researchers use OpenGL to visualize complex data sets, enabling them to better understand and communicate their findings. This includes applications in fields like medical imaging, geology, and climate modeling.

4. Simulations

OpenGL is employed in simulations for training purposes, such as flight simulators and medical simulations. Its ability to render realistic scenes is crucial for creating effective training environments.

5. Multimedia and Entertainment

Beyond gaming, OpenGL is integral to multimedia applications, including video playback, 2D/3D animation, and special effects in movies and television.

Conclusion

OpenGL's history and versatile applications make it a fundamental technology in the world of graphics programming. Its ability to provide high-performance rendering and cross-platform compatibility has solidified its position as a go-to choice for developers across various industries. As we continue our exploration of graphics programming, we will delve deeper into the concepts and techniques that underpin OpenGL, equipping you with the knowledge to create stunning graphics and interactive experiences.

Section 1.3: Introduction to WebGL: The Web's Graphics Language

WebGL, short for Web Graphics Library, has revolutionized the way graphics are rendered in web applications. In this section, we'll dive into WebGL, exploring its origins, capabilities, and how it has become a cornerstone of web-based graphics programming.

The Birth of WebGL

WebGL was born out of the need for powerful, hardware-accelerated graphics within web browsers. Traditional web technologies, such as HTML and CSS, were primarily designed for rendering static content. However, as web applications became more complex and interactive, there was a demand for a means to incorporate dynamic 3D graphics directly into web pages.

WebGL emerged as a solution to this challenge, providing a JavaScript API based on OpenGL ES (Embedded Systems). It enables developers to harness the GPU's capabilities for rendering 2D and 3D graphics within a web browser, opening up a new realm of possibilities for web-based applications.

Key Features of WebGL

WebGL inherits many features from its OpenGL lineage, making it a powerful tool for creating immersive web graphics. Some of its key features include:

1. Hardware Acceleration

WebGL takes advantage of the user's GPU, which significantly boosts rendering performance. This hardware acceleration allows for real-time rendering of complex scenes and animations in web applications.

2. Cross-Platform Compatibility

WebGL is supported by major web browsers, including Chrome, Firefox, Safari, and Edge, making it a cross-platform solution for web developers. This ensures that WebGL content can be experienced consistently across different devices and operating systems.

```
<!—Example HTML to embed a WebGL canvas—>

<!DOCTYPE html>

<html>

<head>

<title>WebGL Example</title>

</head>

<body>

<canvas id="myCanvas" width="800" height="600"></canvas>
```

```
<script src="webgl_script.js"></script>

</body>

</html>
```

3. Integration with HTML and JavaScript

WebGL seamlessly integrates with HTML and JavaScript, allowing developers to create interactive graphics by manipulating the Document Object Model (DOM) and responding to user input events.

```
const canvas = document.getElementById("myCanvas");

const gl = canvas.getContext("webgl");

if (!gl) {

console.error("WebGL not supported, falling back on experimental-webgl");

gl = canvas.getContext("experimental-webgl");

}

if (!gl) {

alert("Your browser does not support WebGL");

}

// WebGL rendering code here

// ...
```

WebGL in Action

WebGL has found applications in various domains, transforming the web into a dynamic and visually engaging platform. Here are some examples of how WebGL is used:

1. Interactive 3D Graphics

WebGL is commonly used to create interactive 3D graphics in web-based games, simulations, and product visualizations. It enables users to explore and interact with 3D environments directly in their web browsers.

2. Data Visualization

Data scientists and researchers use WebGL to visualize complex data sets, such as geographic data, scientific simulations, and financial data. WebGL's rendering capabilities make it possible to convey information effectively through interactive visualizations.

3. Augmented and Virtual Reality

WebGL serves as a foundation for augmented reality (AR) and virtual reality (VR) experiences on the web. It allows users to explore virtual worlds and interact with AR elements without the need for specialized applications or hardware.

Conclusion

WebGL has transformed web development by bringing hardware-accelerated graphics to the browser. Its integration with HTML and JavaScript, coupled with its cross-platform compatibility, has made it a powerful tool for creating immersive web experiences. As we delve deeper into this book, we'll explore the intricacies of WebGL programming and equip you with the knowledge and skills to harness its capabilities effectively.

Section 1.4: Comparing OpenGL and WebGL: Similarities and Differences

In this section, we will compare OpenGL and WebGL, two powerful graphics programming environments, to understand their similarities and differences. While both are used for rendering graphics, they have distinct characteristics and target platforms.

Similarities

1. Graphics Rendering Capabilities

Both OpenGL and WebGL are designed for rendering 2D and 3D graphics. They provide the tools and functions necessary to create visually appealing scenes, manipulate objects, and apply various rendering techniques like shading and texturing.

2. Based on OpenGL

WebGL is, in essence, a subset of OpenGL. It is based on the OpenGL ES specification, which is a simplified version of OpenGL designed for embedded systems like mobile devices. This means that many concepts and functions in WebGL are similar to those in OpenGL, making it easier for developers with OpenGL experience to transition to WebGL.

3. Shader-Based Rendering

Both OpenGL and WebGL embrace shader-based rendering, a modern approach to graphics programming. Shaders are small programs executed on the GPU that control various aspects of the rendering process. This allows for greater flexibility and customization in creating visual effects.

Differences

1. Platform

One of the most significant differences between OpenGL and WebGL is the platform they target. OpenGL is primarily used for desktop applications, running on Windows, macOS, and Linux. In contrast, WebGL is designed specifically for web browsers, enabling graphics rendering directly within web pages.

2. Programming Languages

OpenGL traditionally uses C or C++ as its programming language, while WebGL relies on JavaScript. This language difference reflects the environments they operate in. WebGL leverages the scripting capabilities of web browsers, making it accessible to web developers.

3. Deployment and Distribution

Deploying OpenGL applications typically involves packaging them as standalone desktop applications, which users need to install. WebGL applications, on the other hand, are distributed through web servers and can be accessed instantly through a web browser, eliminating the need for installation.

```
<!—Embedding WebGL in an HTML document—>

<!DOCTYPE html>

<html>

<head>

<title>WebGL Example</title>

</head>

<body>

<canvas id="myCanvas" width="800" height="600"></canvas>

<script src="webgl_script.js"></script>

</body>

</html>
```

4. Security and Sandboxing

WebGL operates within the security constraints of web browsers. This means that WebGL applications are subject to the same security policies as other web content. While this provides a layer of security, it also imposes limitations on what WebGL applications can access and do compared to standalone OpenGL applications.

Choosing Between OpenGL and WebGL

The choice between OpenGL and WebGL depends on the specific requirements of your project and the target platform. If you are developing a traditional desktop application that requires high-performance graphics and has no web-related constraints, OpenGL may be the better choice. On the other hand, if you aim to create web-based interactive graphics or need to reach a broad online audience, WebGL is the way to go.

Understanding the similarities and differences between these two environments will help you make an informed decision and enable you to leverage the strengths of each in your graphics programming endeavors. In the upcoming chapters, we will delve deeper into the specifics of OpenGL and WebGL, providing you with the knowledge and skills needed to excel in both domains.

Section 1.5: The Significance of Bridging OpenGL and WebGL

Bridging the gap between OpenGL and WebGL is a topic of significant importance in modern graphics programming. In this section, we will explore why this integration is crucial and the advantages it brings to developers and the broader technology landscape.

Leveraging Existing Expertise

For developers with experience in OpenGL, transitioning to WebGL or creating web applications can be challenging. Bridging technologies that allow for OpenGL and WebGL integration enable developers to leverage their existing knowledge and skills in both environments. This reduces the learning curve and accelerates the development of web-based graphics applications.

Cross-Platform Compatibility

Bridging technologies enable the creation of cross-platform graphics applications that can run both as native desktop applications using OpenGL and web applications using WebGL. This flexibility is essential for reaching a broader audience and ensuring that your graphics applications are accessible across different devices and operating systems.

```
// Example of a bridging library for OpenGL to WebGL

const gl = require('gl');

// Create an OpenGL context

const glContext = gl(800, 600);

// Use OpenGL functions

glContext.clear(glContext.COLOR_BUFFER_BIT);

// ...

// Convert OpenGL context to WebGL context

const webglContext = glContext.getWebGLContext();

// Use WebGL functions

webglContext.clear(webglContext.COLOR_BUFFER_BIT);

// ...
```

Code Reusability

Bridging technologies allow for code reusability between OpenGL and WebGL applications. This means that developers can write core rendering logic and shaders once and use them across both environments with minimal modification. This not only saves development time but also ensures consistency in graphics rendering.

Performance Optimization

By bridging OpenGL and WebGL, developers can optimize their graphics applications for performance in both contexts. This optimization might involve fine-tuning shaders, utilizing hardware acceleration, and adopting best practices from both environments. The result is graphics applications that perform efficiently, whether running natively or in a web browser.

Extending Application Reach

Integrating OpenGL and WebGL can extend the reach of your graphics applications. For example, you can offer a desktop version of your application with OpenGL for users seeking maximum performance and a web version for broader accessibility. This approach can be particularly beneficial for games, simulations, and data visualization tools.

Challenges in Bridging

While the advantages of bridging OpenGL and WebGL are significant, it's essential to acknowledge the challenges that come with this integration. Ensuring compatibility, handling differences in rendering contexts, and managing resource loading are some of the technical challenges developers may encounter. However, as bridging technologies evolve, these challenges become more manageable, making it increasingly feasible to create seamless transitions between OpenGL and WebGL.

In the upcoming chapters, we will explore tools and libraries that facilitate the integration of OpenGL and WebGL, as well as real-world case studies showcasing successful implementations. Bridging these two graphics environments empowers developers to harness the strengths of both technologies and opens up new possibilities in the world of graphics programming.

Chapter 2: Understanding OpenGL

Section 2.1: Core Concepts of OpenGL

OpenGL, as a graphics programming library, is built upon a set of core concepts that form the foundation of how graphics are rendered and manipulated. In this section, we'll delve into these fundamental concepts to provide you with a solid understanding of OpenGL's inner workings.

Rendering Pipeline

At the heart of OpenGL lies the rendering pipeline. This pipeline is a series of stages through which geometric data is transformed into pixels on the screen. Understanding the stages of the rendering pipeline is crucial for controlling and optimizing the rendering process.

The typical stages of the rendering pipeline include:

1. **Vertex Processing**: This stage processes the input vertices of geometric shapes. It applies transformations like translation, rotation, and scaling to position these vertices in 3D space.
2. **Vertex Shader**: A vertex shader is a programmable stage in which you can manipulate vertex data. It's often used for transformations, lighting calculations, and other per-vertex operations.
3. **Tessellation Control and Evaluation**: These stages are optional and are used for controlling and evaluating tessellation, which subdivides surfaces for smoother rendering.
4. **Geometry Shader**: Another programmable stage that

allows for geometry manipulation, such as adding or removing vertices. It's useful for tasks like particle systems and geometry-based effects.

5. **Rasterization**: In this stage, the 3D primitives are converted into 2D fragments or pixels on the screen. It determines which fragments belong to each primitive and their positions.
6. **Fragment Shader**: The fragment shader is responsible for computing the color of each fragment. It can apply texture mapping, lighting calculations, and other per-fragment operations.
7. **Per-Fragment Operations**: These operations include depth testing, stencil testing, and blending. They determine the final color and depth values of each fragment.
8. **Framebuffer**: The framebuffer stores the final image that will be displayed on the screen. It may include color buffers, depth buffers, and stencil buffers.

State Machine

OpenGL operates as a state machine, which means that it maintains a set of internal states that control various aspects of rendering. These states determine how OpenGL behaves when rendering objects. Some common OpenGL states include the current shader program, the current texture, and the current viewport.

Developers can change these states using OpenGL functions, and these changes persist until explicitly modified. Understanding and managing the OpenGL state machine is essential for achieving the desired rendering outcomes.

Shaders

Shaders are small programs written in GLSL (OpenGL Shading Language) that run on the GPU. They are used to control various aspects of the rendering process. There are two main types of shaders in OpenGL:

1. **Vertex Shader**: As mentioned earlier, the vertex shader operates on individual vertices and can perform transformations, lighting calculations, and other per-vertex operations.
2. **Fragment Shader**: The fragment shader, also known as the pixel shader, operates on individual fragments (pixels) and determines their final color based on factors like lighting, textures, and material properties.

Shaders provide a high degree of customization and flexibility, allowing developers to implement complex rendering techniques and achieve realistic graphics.

Buffers and Objects

OpenGL relies on various buffers and objects to store and manage data efficiently. Some of the most commonly used ones include:

1. **Vertex Buffer Objects (VBOs)**: These store vertex data, such as positions, normals, and texture coordinates, on the GPU. VBOs reduce the need for frequent data transfers between the CPU and GPU.
2. **Element Buffer Objects (EBOs)**: EBOs store indices that reference vertices in VBOs, allowing for efficient reuse of vertices in multiple primitives.
3. **Framebuffers**: Framebuffers are used to render to off-screen targets, enabling techniques like shadow mapping,

post-processing effects, and render-to-texture.

4. **Textures**: Textures are used to apply images or patterns to surfaces, adding realism to 3D objects. They are commonly used for materials, environment mapping, and other effects.
5. **Shader Programs**: Shader programs consist of vertex and fragment shaders. They define how vertex data is processed and how fragments are shaded. Shader programs are a crucial part of OpenGL's programmable pipeline.

Understanding how to create, manage, and use these buffers and objects is essential for efficient OpenGL programming.

Coordinate Systems

OpenGL uses a right-handed coordinate system, where the X-axis points to the right, the Y-axis points up, and the Z-axis points out of the screen toward the viewer. This coordinate system is essential for understanding how transformations, projections, and camera views affect the rendering of objects in 3D space.

Conclusion

These core concepts of OpenGL lay the groundwork for more advanced graphics programming. By grasping the rendering pipeline, the state machine, shaders, buffers, and coordinate systems, you'll have a solid foundation for working with OpenGL and creating impressive 3D graphics. In the chapters that follow, we will delve deeper into each of these concepts and explore practical examples and techniques for harnessing the power of OpenGL.

Section 2.2: OpenGL Architecture and Pipeline

To work effectively with OpenGL, it's essential to understand its architecture and the stages of the rendering pipeline. In this section, we'll explore the internal architecture of OpenGL and how data flows through its rendering pipeline.

OpenGL Architecture

OpenGL is designed as a platform-independent graphics library. It acts as an intermediary between your application and the underlying graphics hardware, allowing you to write code that works across various operating systems and hardware configurations.

OpenGL Implementations

OpenGL is not a standalone software package but rather a specification that different hardware vendors implement. These implementations, often referred to as OpenGL drivers, provide the interface between your application and the graphics hardware. Popular OpenGL implementations include NVIDIA's GeForce drivers, AMD's Radeon Software, and Intel's Mesa drivers.

OpenGL API

The OpenGL API (Application Programming Interface) consists of a set of functions and constants that you can use in your application to interact with the OpenGL driver and hardware. These functions cover a wide range of tasks, from creating and managing OpenGL objects to specifying rendering parameters and issuing drawing commands.

Rendering Pipeline Overview

The OpenGL rendering pipeline is a series of stages that process geometric data and produce the final rendered image. Let's briefly overview the primary stages of the rendering pipeline:

1. **Vertex Processing**: The pipeline starts with vertex data, which can represent the position, color, normal, and other attributes of vertices in 3D space. Vertex data is processed through various stages, including vertex transformation, tessellation, and geometry shading.
2. **Primitive Assembly**: After vertex processing, primitive assembly combines vertices into geometric primitives like points, lines, and triangles. These primitives are then sent for rasterization.
3. **Rasterization**: Rasterization converts the geometric primitives into fragments or pixels on the screen. It determines which fragments are inside the view frustum and are thus part of the final image.
4. **Fragment Processing**: Fragments generated during rasterization are processed by fragment shaders. Fragment shaders determine the final color of each fragment based on factors like lighting, texturing, and material properties.
5. **Per-Fragment Operations**: After fragment processing, per-fragment operations like depth testing, stencil testing, and blending are applied. These operations determine the final values for each fragment's color, depth, and other attributes.
6. **Framebuffer**: The final fragments are written to the framebuffer, which is essentially the screen or an off-screen target. The framebuffer may consist of color buffers, depth buffers, and stencil buffers, depending on the rendering needs.

OpenGL Versions

OpenGL has evolved over the years, with different versions introducing new features and capabilities. Some of the most notable versions include:

- **OpenGL 1.x**: The original version of OpenGL, with fixed-function pipeline graphics rendering.
- **OpenGL 2.0**: Introduced programmable shaders, allowing for greater flexibility in graphics rendering.
- **OpenGL 3.0 and Later**: Transitioned to a fully programmable pipeline, removing the fixed-function pipeline. These versions provide more control and flexibility but require shader programming expertise.
- **OpenGL ES**: A subset of OpenGL designed for embedded systems, such as mobile devices and web browsers. WebGL is based on OpenGL ES.
- **OpenGL Core Profile**: A subset of modern OpenGL versions that removes deprecated features, focusing on the core graphics functionality.
- **OpenGL Compatibility Profile**: Includes both modern and deprecated features, providing backward compatibility for older OpenGL applications.

Understanding the OpenGL pipeline and the differences between OpenGL versions is essential for choosing the right approach for your graphics programming needs. Whether you're working with legacy OpenGL or the latest versions, these fundamental concepts remain at the core of OpenGL development.

Section 2.3: Setting Up an OpenGL Environment

Before you can start programming with OpenGL, it's crucial to set up the development environment correctly. In this section, we'll guide you through the steps required to set up an OpenGL development environment on your computer.

Choose a Programming Language

OpenGL itself is not a programming language but rather a library of functions and constants. To work with OpenGL, you'll need to choose a programming language in which you'll write your code. Common languages used with OpenGL include C, C++, and more recently, Python and Rust. The choice of language often depends on your project's requirements and your personal preferences.

Install a Compiler

If you haven't already, you'll need a compiler for your chosen programming language. Popular choices include:

- **C/C++**: GCC (GNU Compiler Collection) for Linux, MinGW for Windows, Xcode for macOS.

- **Python**: Python comes with its interpreter, so you typically don't need a separate compiler.

- **Rust**: Install Rust and Cargo, the Rust package manager, which includes the Rust compiler.

Ensure your compiler is properly installed and configured before proceeding.

Set Up an OpenGL Context

OpenGL requires a rendering context to interface with your graphics hardware. The setup process for an OpenGL context varies depending on your programming language and platform. Here's a simplified example in C++ using the GLFW library:

```
#include <GL/glew.h>

#include <GLFW/glfw3.h>

int main() {

// Initialize GLFW

if (!glfwInit()) {

return -1;

}

// Create a GLFW window and OpenGL context

GLFWwindow* window = glfwCreateWindow(800, 600, "OpenGL Window", NULL, NULL);

if (!window) {

glfwTerminate();

return -1;

}

// Make the OpenGL context current

glfwMakeContextCurrent(window);

// Initialize GLEW (OpenGL Extension Wrangler)
```

```
if (glewInit() != GLEW_OK) {
glfwTerminate();
return -1;
}
// Now you have an OpenGL context ready for rendering
// Main rendering loop
while (!glfwWindowShouldClose(window)) {
// Render your graphics here
// Swap front and back buffers
glfwSwapBuffers(window);
// Poll for and process events
glfwPollEvents();
}
// Clean up and exit
glfwTerminate();
return 0;
}
```

Install OpenGL Libraries

To use OpenGL functions in your code, you'll need to link against the appropriate OpenGL libraries. The exact process for this depends on your development environment. For example, in C/C++, you might use libraries like GLEW (OpenGL Extension Wrangler) to manage OpenGL extensions and dependencies.

Create a Simple OpenGL Program

To verify that your OpenGL environment is set up correctly, create a simple OpenGL program that opens a window and clears it with a specific color. This serves as a basic test of your development environment:

```
#include <GL/glew.h>

#include <GLFW/glfw3.h>

int main() {

// Initialize GLFW

if (!glfwInit()) {

return -1;

}

// Create a GLFW window and OpenGL context

GLFWwindow* window = glfwCreateWindow(800, 600, "OpenGL Window", NULL, NULL);

if (!window) {

glfwTerminate();

return -1;

}

// Make the OpenGL context current
```

```
glfwMakeContextCurrent(window);
// Initialize GLEW (OpenGL Extension Wrangler)
if (glewInit() != GLEW_OK) {
glfwTerminate();
return -1;
}
// Set the clear color (R, G, B, A)
glClearColor(0.0f, 0.0f, 0.0f, 1.0f);
// Main rendering loop
while (!glfwWindowShouldClose(window)) {
// Clear the color buffer
glClear(GL_COLOR_BUFFER_BIT);
// Render your graphics here
// Swap front and back buffers
glfwSwapBuffers(window);
// Poll for and process events
glfwPollEvents();
}
// Clean up and exit
glfwTerminate();
```

```
return 0;

}
```

Running this program should open a window with a black background. If it does, your OpenGL development environment is set up correctly, and you're ready to start exploring OpenGL programming in more depth.

Section 2.4: Basic OpenGL Programming Techniques

Now that you have your OpenGL environment set up, let's dive into some fundamental OpenGL programming techniques. In this section, we'll cover the basics of rendering geometric shapes, applying transformations, and working with shaders.

Rendering a Triangle

Rendering a triangle is often the first step in OpenGL programming. It serves as a simple yet powerful introduction to OpenGL's capabilities. Here's a minimal example of how to render a colored triangle in OpenGL using C++ and GLFW:

```
#include <GL/glew.h>

#include <GLFW/glfw3.h>

int main() {

// Initialize GLFW

if (!glfwInit()) {

return -1;
```

```
}
// Create a GLFW window and OpenGL context
GLFWwindow* window = glfwCreateWindow(800, 600, "OpenGL Triangle", NULL, NULL);
if (!window) {
glfwTerminate();
return -1;
}
// Make the OpenGL context current
glfwMakeContextCurrent(window);
// Initialize GLEW (OpenGL Extension Wrangler)
if (glewInit() != GLEW_OK) {
glfwTerminate();
return -1;
}
// Define the vertices of the triangle
float vertices[] = {
-0.5f, -0.5f, 0.0f, // Vertex 1 (x, y, z)
0.5f, -0.5f, 0.0f, // Vertex 2 (x, y, z)
0.0f, 0.5f, 0.0f // Vertex 3 (x, y, z)
};
```

```
// Create a Vertex Buffer Object (VBO)

GLuint VBO;

glGenBuffers(1, &VBO);

glBindBuffer(GL_ARRAY_BUFFER, VBO);

glBufferData(GL_ARRAY_BUFFER, sizeof(vertices), vertices, GL_STATIC_DRAW);

// Vertex Shader

const char* vertexShaderSource = R"(

#version 330 core

layout (location = 0) in vec3 aPos;

void main() {

gl_Position = vec4(aPos.x, aPos.y, aPos.z, 1.0);

}

)";

// Fragment Shader

const char* fragmentShaderSource = R"(

#version 330 core

out vec4 FragColor;

void main() {

FragColor = vec4(1.0f, 0.5f, 0.2f, 1.0f);

}
```

```
)";
// Compile and link shaders
// (Code for shader compilation and linking not shown here)
// Main rendering loop
while (!glfwWindowShouldClose(window)) {
// Clear the color buffer
glClear(GL_COLOR_BUFFER_BIT);
// Bind the shader program
glUseProgram(shaderProgram);
// Bind the VBO
glBindBuffer(GL_ARRAY_BUFFER, VBO);
// Enable the "aPos" attribute
glEnableVertexAttribArray(0);
glVertexAttribPointer(0, 3, GL_FLOAT, GL_FALSE, 3 * sizeof(float), (void*)0);
// Draw the triangle
glDrawArrays(GL_TRIANGLES, 0, 3);
// Disable the "aPos" attribute
glDisableVertexAttribArray(0);
// Swap front and back buffers
glfwSwapBuffers(window);
```

```
// Poll for and process events
glfwPollEvents();
}
// Clean up and exit
glfwTerminate();
return 0;
}
```

This code sets up a basic OpenGL program that renders a colored triangle. It defines the triangle's vertices, creates a Vertex Buffer Object (VBO) to store the vertex data, and compiles simple vertex and fragment shaders. The shaders specify the vertex positions and fragment color.

Transformation Matrices

Transformations are essential in OpenGL to position, scale, and rotate objects in 3D space. OpenGL uses transformation matrices to achieve these transformations. Common transformations include translation, rotation, and scaling. Here's a brief overview:

- **Translation**: Moving an object from one position to another in space.
- **Rotation**: Rotating an object around a specified axis.
- **Scaling**: Changing the size of an object along its axes.

Transformation matrices are applied to the vertices of objects before rendering, allowing you to control their placement and orientation in the 3D scene.

Shaders

In the previous example, we briefly introduced shaders, which are essential components of modern OpenGL programming. Shaders are small programs that run on the GPU and control various aspects of rendering. They are typically written in GLSL (OpenGL Shading Language).

- **Vertex Shader**: Processes individual vertices and can perform transformations, lighting calculations, and other per-vertex operations.

- **Fragment Shader**: Determines the final color of each fragment (pixel) in the rendered image. It can apply texture mapping, lighting calculations, and other per-fragment operations.

Creating and managing shaders is a critical aspect of OpenGL programming, and shaders provide a high degree of customization and control over the rendering process.

Conclusion

These basic OpenGL programming techniques serve as a starting point for your journey into graphics programming. By rendering a simple triangle, understanding transformation matrices, and working with shaders, you've laid the foundation for more advanced OpenGL applications. In the following chapters, we'll explore more complex rendering techniques, lighting, textures, and advanced OpenGL features.

Section 2.5: Advanced Features in OpenGL

In this section, we'll delve into some advanced features and techniques that you can leverage when working with OpenGL. These capabilities allow you to create more sophisticated and visually appealing graphics.

Multiple Objects and Transformations

In many OpenGL applications, you'll need to render multiple objects with different positions, orientations, and scales. To achieve this, you can apply transformations selectively before rendering each object. By managing transformation matrices for each object, you can create complex scenes with various entities.

```
// Pseudocode for rendering multiple objects with transformations

for each object {

// Apply the object's model matrix (combination of translation, rotation, and scale)

setModelMatrix(object.transform);

// Bind the object's VBO

glBindBuffer(GL_ARRAY_BUFFER, object.VBO);

// Enable and set vertex attributes

glEnableVertexAttribArray(0);

glVertexAttribPointer(0, 3, GL_FLOAT, GL_FALSE, 3 * sizeof(float), (void*)0);

// Draw the object
```

```
glDrawArrays(GL_TRIANGLES, 0, object.vertexCount);

// Disable vertex attributes

glDisableVertexAttribArray(0);

}
```

Depth Testing and Z-Buffer

To handle the visibility of objects in 3D scenes, OpenGL provides depth testing and a Z-buffer (depth buffer). The depth buffer stores depth values for each pixel on the screen. When rendering, depth testing compares the depth of each fragment to the depth stored in the depth buffer. Fragments that pass the depth test are drawn, while others are discarded.

```
// Enable depth testing

glEnable(GL_DEPTH_TEST);

// Main rendering loop

while (!glfwWindowShouldClose(window)) {

// Clear color and depth buffers

glClear(GL_COLOR_BUFFER_BIT |
GL_DEPTH_BUFFER_BIT);

// Render objects with transformations

// Swap front and back buffers

glfwSwapBuffers(window);

// Poll for and process events
```

```
glfwPollEvents();

}
```

Blending and Transparency

Blending allows you to create transparent and semi-transparent objects by controlling the alpha (transparency) value of fragments. You can specify how incoming fragment colors are combined with the existing colors in the framebuffer. Common blending modes include alpha blending for transparency and additive blending for special effects.

```
// Enable blending

glEnable(GL_BLEND);

glBlendFunc(GL_SRC_ALPHA,
GL_ONE_MINUS_SRC_ALPHA);

// Render transparent objects
```

Framebuffers and Off-Screen Rendering

OpenGL allows you to render scenes to off-screen framebuffers instead of directly to the screen. This technique is useful for post-processing effects, shadow mapping, and rendering to textures. You can create and bind custom framebuffers to render scenes into textures, which can then be used in subsequent rendering passes.

```
// Create and bind a custom framebuffer

GLuint framebuffer;

glGenFramebuffers(1, &framebuffer);

glBindFramebuffer(GL_FRAMEBUFFER, framebuffer);
```

```
// Attach a texture as the color buffer for this framebuffer

GLuint texture;

glGenTextures(1, &texture);

glBindTexture(GL_TEXTURE_2D, texture);

glTexImage2D(GL_TEXTURE_2D, 0, GL_RGB, width, height, 0,
GL_RGB, GL_UNSIGNED_BYTE, NULL);

glFramebufferTexture2D(GL_FRAMEBUFFER,
GL_COLOR_ATTACHMENT0, GL_TEXTURE_2D, texture,
0);

// Render scene to the custom framebuffer

// ...

// Bind the default framebuffer (screen)

glBindFramebuffer(GL_FRAMEBUFFER, 0);

// Use the texture in subsequent rendering passes
```

Advanced Shading Techniques

Advanced shading techniques enhance the realism and visual quality of rendered scenes. These include:

- **Phong Shading**: A shading model that simulates specular highlights for smoother and more realistic surfaces.
- **Normal Mapping**: A technique that adds fine details to surfaces without increasing geometry complexity by modifying surface normals.

- **Shadow Mapping**: Simulating shadows cast by objects in the scene, creating depth and realism.

- **Environment Mapping**: Rendering reflections and refractions by mapping the environment onto objects.

- **Deferred Shading**: A rendering technique that separates lighting calculations from the geometry pass, enabling more complex lighting models.

These advanced techniques often require more complex shader programs and careful consideration of scene rendering.

Tessellation and Geometry Shaders

Tessellation and geometry shaders provide powerful tools for advanced graphics rendering. Tessellation shaders allow for dynamic subdivision of surfaces, enabling smoother and more detailed surfaces. Geometry shaders can manipulate primitives, add or remove vertices, and create complex geometry-based effects.

```
// Example of tessellation control and evaluation shaders

// (Code for shaders not shown here)

// Enable tessellation

glEnable(GL_TESSATION);
```

Compute Shaders

Compute shaders are a separate type of shader in OpenGL that perform general-purpose computing tasks on the GPU. They are not part of the rendering pipeline but can be used for tasks like physics simulations, data processing, and parallel computations.

```
// Example of using a compute shader
// (Code for compute shader not shown here)
glUseProgram(computeShaderProgram);
glDispatchCompute(numGroupsX, numGroupsY, numGroupsZ);
glMemoryBarrier(GL_SHADER_STORAGE_BARRIER_BIT);
```

These advanced features and techniques open up a world of possibilities in OpenGL programming, allowing you to create visually stunning and interactive 3D graphics applications. As you explore these capabilities, keep in mind that mastering them may require a deeper understanding of OpenGL and shader programming.

Chapter 3: Diving into WebGL

Section 3.1: Fundamentals of WebGL

WebGL, short for Web Graphics Library, is a JavaScript API for rendering interactive 3D and 2D graphics within web browsers without the need for plugins. It is based on OpenGL ES (Embedded Systems) and brings the power of hardware-accelerated graphics to the web platform. In this section, we will explore the fundamentals of WebGL, its architecture, and the core concepts you need to understand to start working with it effectively.

WebGL Architecture

WebGL is designed to work seamlessly with web technologies such as HTML, CSS, and JavaScript. It enables you to create interactive graphics and animations directly in the browser. Let's briefly examine the key components of WebGL architecture:

- **HTML**: WebGL content is embedded within HTML documents using the <canvas> element. This element serves as the drawing surface for WebGL graphics.

- **JavaScript**: JavaScript is used to interact with the WebGL API. You can write JavaScript code to initialize WebGL, send commands to the GPU, and handle user interactions.

- **WebGL API**: The WebGL API provides a set of JavaScript functions and objects that allow you to control the rendering process. It closely resembles the OpenGL ES API, making it familiar to developers with experience in graphics programming.

- **GPU**: WebGL leverages the power of the graphics processing unit (GPU) to accelerate graphics rendering. It allows you to offload complex rendering tasks to the GPU, resulting in better performance and smoother animations.

WebGL Rendering Context

To begin working with WebGL, you need to create a WebGL rendering context. The rendering context is the bridge between your JavaScript code and the GPU. Here's how you can obtain a WebGL rendering context:

```
// Get a reference to the <canvas> element in your HTML document

const canvas = document.getElementById('myCanvas');

// Get the WebGL rendering context for the canvas

const gl = canvas.getContext('webgl');

if (!gl) {

console.error('WebGL is not supported on this browser.');

}
```

The WebGL Rendering Pipeline

WebGL follows a rendering pipeline similar to traditional OpenGL. Understanding this pipeline is essential for creating and manipulating graphics in WebGL. The primary stages of the WebGL rendering pipeline include:

1. **Vertex Processing**: In this stage, you provide vertex data that describes the geometry of your 3D objects. This data is

processed through vertex shaders, which are small programs that run on the GPU for each vertex. Vertex shaders can perform transformations, lighting calculations, and other operations on the vertices.

2. **Primitive Assembly**: After vertex processing, the WebGL pipeline assembles vertices into primitive shapes like points, lines, and triangles.
3. **Rasterization**: Rasterization converts primitive shapes into fragments or pixels on the screen. It determines which fragments are within the view frustum and should be part of the final image.
4. **Fragment Processing**: Fragment shaders are executed for each fragment generated during rasterization. These shaders determine the final color of each fragment based on factors like lighting, textures, and material properties.
5. **Per-Fragment Operations**: After fragment processing, per-fragment operations like depth testing, blending, and stencil testing are applied. These operations determine the final values for each fragment's color, depth, and other attributes.
6. **Framebuffer**: The final fragments are written to the framebuffer, which represents the screen or an off-screen rendering target. You can render to off-screen framebuffers to create post-processing effects or complex scenes.

WebGL Versions

WebGL has multiple versions, primarily WebGL 1.0 and WebGL 2.0. WebGL 2.0 is more feature-rich and powerful, but WebGL 1.0 is more widely supported across various web browsers. The choice between these versions depends on your project's requirements and target audience.

Conclusion

WebGL provides a powerful way to create interactive and visually appealing graphics within web browsers. Understanding its architecture and the rendering pipeline is the first step in becoming proficient in WebGL programming. In the following sections of this chapter, we will explore setting up a WebGL environment, basic WebGL programming techniques, and leveraging WebGL for advanced graphics on the web.

Section 3.2: The WebGL Rendering Pipeline

In this section, we'll take a deeper dive into the WebGL rendering pipeline, which is at the core of rendering 3D and 2D graphics in WebGL. Understanding how this pipeline works is crucial for effectively using WebGL to create interactive web graphics.

Vertex Shaders in WebGL

Vertex shaders in WebGL are responsible for processing individual vertices and are written in GLSL (OpenGL Shading Language). Here's a simple example of a vertex shader in WebGL:

```
// Vertex Shader

attribute vec4 a_position; // Input attribute for vertex position

uniform mat4 u_modelViewMatrix; // Model-View matrix uniform

void main() {

// Apply the model-view matrix to the vertex position

gl_Position = u_modelViewMatrix * a_position;

}
```

- The attribute keyword defines an input attribute for the vertex position, which will be provided by your JavaScript code.

- The uniform keyword indicates a uniform variable that is set from JavaScript, such as the model-view matrix used for transformations.

- The main() function is the entry point for the vertex shader, where you perform operations on the vertex positions. In this example, we apply the model-view matrix to the input vertex position.

Fragment Shaders in WebGL

Fragment shaders determine the final color of each fragment (pixel) in the rendered image. Here's a simple example of a fragment shader in WebGL:

```
// Fragment Shader

precision mediump float; // Specify the precision of floating-point calculations

void main() {

// Set the fragment color to red (R, G, B, A)

gl_FragColor = vec4(1.0, 0.0, 0.0, 1.0);

}
```

- The precision keyword specifies the precision of floating-point calculations in the fragment shader. In this case, mediump is used, which is a medium precision level.

• The main() function is where you determine the final color of the fragment. In this simple example, we set the color to red (R=1.0, G=0.0, B=0.0, A=1.0).

Vertex Buffers and Attributes

In WebGL, you need to create and manage vertex buffers to store vertex data, which includes positions, normals, colors, and other attributes. You also define how these attributes are passed to the vertex shader.

Here's an example of setting up vertex data and attributes in WebGL:

```
// Define vertex data

const vertices = [

0.0, 0.0, 0.0, // Vertex 1

1.0, 0.0, 0.0, // Vertex 2

0.5, 1.0, 0.0 // Vertex 3

];

// Create a buffer for the vertex data

const vertexBuffer = gl.createBuffer();

gl.bindBuffer(gl.ARRAY_BUFFER, vertexBuffer);

gl.bufferData(gl.ARRAY_BUFFER, new Float32Array(vertices), gl.STATIC_DRAW);

// Get the attribute location in the shader

const positionAttributeLocation = gl.getAttribLocation(program, 'a_position');
```

// Enable the attribute

gl.enableVertexAttribArray(positionAttributeLocation);

// Point an attribute to the currently bound VBO

gl.bindBuffer(gl.ARRAY_BUFFER, vertexBuffer);

gl.vertexAttribPointer(positionAttributeLocation, 3, gl.FLOAT, **false**, 0, 0);

- You define your vertex data as an array and create a buffer to store it.
- You get the attribute location from your shader program using gl.getAttribLocation().
- The attribute is enabled using gl.enableVertexAttribArray().
- Finally, you bind the buffer and point the attribute to the data in the buffer using gl.vertexAttribPointer().

WebGL Rendering Loop

In WebGL, you typically use a rendering loop to continuously update and redraw the scene. This loop repeatedly calls a function that contains your rendering code.

function render() {

// Clear the canvas

gl.clear(gl.COLOR_BUFFER_BIT);

// Set uniforms and draw objects

```
// ...
// Request the next frame
requestAnimationFrame(render);
}
// Start the rendering loop
render();
```

The requestAnimationFrame() function is used to schedule the next frame, ensuring smooth and efficient animations.

WebGL Framebuffers

WebGL allows you to create off-screen framebuffers for rendering. This is useful for post-processing effects, shadow mapping, and more. You can render a scene to a texture attached to a framebuffer and then use that texture in subsequent rendering passes.

```
// Create and bind a framebuffer
const framebuffer = gl.createFramebuffer();
gl.bindFramebuffer(gl.FRAMEBUFFER, framebuffer);
// Create and attach a texture to the framebuffer as the color buffer
const texture = gl.createTexture();
gl.bindTexture(gl.TEXTURE_2D, texture);
gl.texImage2D(gl.TEXTURE_2D, 0, gl.RGBA, width, height, 0, gl.RGBA, gl.UNSIGNED_BYTE, null);
```

```
gl.framebufferTexture2D(gl.FRAMEBUFFER,
gl.COLOR_ATTACHMENT0, gl.TEXTURE_2D, texture, 0);

// Render to the framebuffer

// ...

// Bind the default framebuffer (screen)

gl.bindFramebuffer(gl.FRAMEBUFFER, null);

// Use the texture in subsequent rendering passes
```

This allows you

Section 3.3: Setting Up a WebGL Environment

Setting up a WebGL environment is the first step to start working with WebGL effectively. In this section, we'll walk through the essential components and steps needed to establish a WebGL environment for creating interactive 3D and 2D graphics within a web browser.

HTML Canvas Element

The HTML <canvas> element is the foundation of your WebGL environment. It serves as the drawing surface where you'll render your graphics. To set up a canvas element, create it within your HTML document:

```
<canvas id="myCanvas" width="800" height="600"></canvas>
```

In this example, we've created a canvas element with an id of "myCanvas" and specified its width and height attributes. You can adjust these dimensions to match your application's requirements.

Obtaining a WebGL Rendering Context

To work with WebGL, you need to obtain a WebGL rendering context from the canvas element. This context is responsible for interacting with the GPU and executing WebGL commands. Here's how you can obtain a WebGL rendering context using JavaScript:

```
const canvas = document.getElementById('myCanvas');

const gl = canvas.getContext('webgl'); // Get the WebGL rendering context

if (!gl) {

console.error('WebGL is not supported on this browser.');

} else {

console.log('WebGL context obtained successfully.');

}
```

In the code above, we first obtain a reference to the canvas element using its id. Then, we use the getContext('webgl') method to request the WebGL rendering context. It's important to check whether WebGL is supported by the browser, as indicated by the presence of a valid context.

WebGL Fundamentals

To begin rendering in WebGL, you need to understand some fundamental concepts:

- **Viewport**: The viewport defines the region of the canvas where the rendering occurs. You can set the viewport's dimensions using WebGL functions like gl.viewport().

- **Coordinate System**: WebGL uses a 3D coordinate system where the origin (0, 0, 0) is typically at the center of the canvas. The X-axis extends to the right, the Y-axis goes up, and the Z-axis comes out of the screen towards you.

- **Buffers**: Buffers are used to store data that will be sent to the GPU. WebGL provides two types of buffers: vertex buffers for storing vertex data and index buffers for specifying the order in which vertices are drawn.

- **Shaders**: Shaders are small programs written in GLSL (OpenGL Shading Language) that run on the GPU. You need at least two shaders: a vertex shader and a fragment shader.

- **Rendering Loop**: WebGL animations are typically implemented using a rendering loop. This loop repeatedly clears the canvas and renders the scene.

Conclusion

Setting up a WebGL environment involves creating an HTML canvas element, obtaining a WebGL rendering context, and understanding fundamental WebGL concepts. In the following sections, we will explore how to use this environment to create and render 3D graphics, work with shaders, and build interactive web applications.

Section 3.4: WebGL Programming Basics

In this section, we'll delve into the basics of programming with WebGL. You'll learn how to create and render simple graphics, set up shaders, and work with buffers and attributes. This foundational knowledge is crucial for building more complex WebGL applications.

Drawing a Triangle

The simplest WebGL program involves drawing a triangle on the canvas. To achieve this, you need to perform the following steps:

1. **Define Vertex Data:** Create an array to store the vertices of the triangle.

```
const vertices = [
0.0, 1.0, 0.0, // Vertex 1 (x, y, z)
-1.0, -1.0, 0.0, // Vertex 2 (x, y, z)
1.0, -1.0, 0.0 // Vertex 3 (x, y, z)
];
```

1. **Create a Vertex Buffer**: Generate a buffer on the GPU and populate it with the vertex data.

```
const vertexBuffer = gl.createBuffer();
gl.bindBuffer(gl.ARRAY_BUFFER, vertexBuffer);
gl.bufferData(gl.ARRAY_BUFFER, new Float32Array(vertices), gl.STATIC_DRAW);
```

1. **Create Shaders:** Write vertex and fragment shaders and compile them.

```
const vertexShaderSource = `
```

```
attribute vec4 a_position;

void main() {

gl_Position = a_position;

}

`;

const fragmentShaderSource = `

void main() {

gl_FragColor = vec4(1.0, 0.0, 0.0, 1.0); // Red color

}

`;

const vertexShader = createShader(gl, gl.VERTEX_SHADER, vertexShaderSource);

const fragmentShader = createShader(gl, gl.FRAGMENT_SHADER, fragmentShaderSource);
```

1. **Link Shaders and Create a Program**: Link the shaders into a shader program.

```
const shaderProgram = gl.createProgram();

gl.attachShader(shaderProgram, vertexShader);

gl.attachShader(shaderProgram, fragmentShader);

gl.linkProgram(shaderProgram);

gl.useProgram(shaderProgram);
```

1. **Define Vertex Attributes**: Specify how the vertex data is structured and connected to the shader program.

```
const positionAttributeLocation = gl.getAttribLocation(shaderProgram, 'a_position');

gl.enableVertexAttribArray(positionAttributeLocation);

gl.bindBuffer(gl.ARRAY_BUFFER, vertexBuffer);

gl.vertexAttribPointer(positionAttributeLocation, 3, gl.FLOAT, false, 0, 0);
```

1. **Render the Triangle**: Use the gl.drawArrays() function to render the triangle.

```
gl.clear(gl.COLOR_BUFFER_BIT);

gl.drawArrays(gl.TRIANGLES, 0, 3);
```

Understanding Shaders

Shaders are the heart of WebGL programming. They consist of two main types:

- **Vertex Shader**: Responsible for processing each vertex's position. It often applies transformations, like scaling, rotation, and translation.
- **Fragment Shader**: Determines the final color of each pixel (fragment) in the triangle. It can incorporate lighting, textures, and other effects.

Shaders are written in GLSL, a C-like language designed for parallel processing on the GPU.

WebGL States

WebGL maintains various states that affect rendering. Two important states are:

- **Viewport**: You can set the viewport's dimensions using gl.viewport(x, y, width, height) to control where rendering occurs on the canvas.

- **Clearing the Canvas**: Before rendering a frame, it's common to clear the canvas using gl.clear(gl.COLOR_BUFFER_BIT) to set the background color.

WebGL Utilities

To simplify WebGL programming, you can create utility functions and libraries. Common tasks involve loading textures, handling user input, and managing complex scenes.

Conclusion

This section introduced you to the fundamentals of WebGL programming, including drawing a simple triangle, working with shaders, and understanding WebGL states. As you become more proficient in WebGL, you'll explore advanced graphics techniques, handle user interaction, and build interactive web applications.

Section 3.5: Leveraging WebGL for Advanced Graphics

WebGL provides a powerful platform for creating advanced graphics on the web. In this section, we'll explore how to leverage

WebGL's capabilities to achieve more sophisticated visual effects and interactivity in your web applications.

Textures

Textures play a vital role in enhancing the realism of 3D scenes. They allow you to apply images to 3D objects, creating surfaces that simulate materials like wood, metal, or fabric. To work with textures in WebGL, you need to:

1. **Load Textures**: Load image textures, such as JPEG or PNG files, into WebGL using functions like gl.texImage2D().
2. **Texture Coordinates**: Define texture coordinates for each vertex of your 3D objects. These coordinates determine how the texture is mapped onto the object's surface.
3. **Shader Uniforms**: Pass texture information to your fragment shader as uniforms. In the fragment shader, you sample the texture to determine the fragment's color.

Here's a simplified example of applying a texture to a triangle:

```
// Load a texture

const texture = gl.createTexture();

gl.bindTexture(gl.TEXTURE_2D, texture);

gl.texImage2D(gl.TEXTURE_2D, 0, gl.RGBA, gl.RGBA, gl.UNSIGNED_BYTE, image);

gl.generateMipmap(gl.TEXTURE_2D);

// Set up texture coordinates

const texCoords = [
```

```
0.0, 0.0,

1.0, 0.0,

0.5, 1.0

];

// Bind and populate the texture coordinate buffer

const texCoordBuffer = gl.createBuffer();

gl.bindBuffer(gl.ARRAY_BUFFER, texCoordBuffer);

gl.bufferData(gl.ARRAY_BUFFER, new Float32Array(texCoords), gl.STATIC_DRAW);

// In the fragment shader, sample the texture using the texture coordinates
```

Lighting and Shadows

Realistic lighting is crucial for creating immersive 3D graphics. WebGL allows you to implement various lighting models, including Phong and Blinn-Phong, to simulate how light interacts with surfaces. You can achieve effects like diffuse reflection, specular highlights, and shadows.

Shadow mapping is a technique used to render shadows in 3D scenes. It involves rendering the scene from the perspective of the light source to create a depth map. This depth map is then used to determine which parts of the scene are in shadow.

Implementing lighting and shadows in WebGL requires understanding shader programming and performing calculations based on the position of lights and objects in the scene.

Post-Processing Effects

WebGL can be used to create stunning post-processing effects, such as depth of field, motion blur, and bloom. These effects are applied to the final rendered image, enhancing its visual appeal.

Post-processing effects are typically achieved by rendering the scene to an off-screen framebuffer, applying one or more shader passes to the rendered image, and then displaying the result on the canvas.

Here's a simplified example of applying a basic post-processing effect (e.g., grayscale) to a scene:

```
// Create an off-screen framebuffer and texture

const framebuffer = gl.createFramebuffer();

gl.bindFramebuffer(gl.FRAMEBUFFER, framebuffer);

const texture = gl.createTexture();

gl.bindTexture(gl.TEXTURE_2D, texture);

gl.texImage2D(gl.TEXTURE_2D, 0, gl.RGBA, gl.RGBA, gl.UNSIGNED_BYTE, null);

gl.framebufferTexture2D(gl.FRAMEBUFFER, gl.COLOR_ATTACHMENT0, gl.TEXTURE_2D, texture, 0);

// Render the scene to the framebuffer

// Apply a post-processing shader pass

// Display the result on the canvas
```

Interactivity

WebGL applications often require user interaction, such as mouse or touch input for camera control, object selection, or interactive animations. You can capture user input events and update the WebGL scene accordingly.

Popular libraries like Three.js provide abstractions for handling user input, making it easier to create interactive 3D applications.

Conclusion

WebGL empowers web developers to create advanced graphics and interactive 3D experiences within web browsers. By understanding how to work with textures, implement lighting and shadows, apply post-processing effects, and handle user interactivity, you can push the boundaries of what's possible in web-based graphics programming. As you explore these advanced techniques, you'll be able to create captivating and immersive web applications.

Chapter 4: The Graphics Pipeline Explained

Section 4.1: Understanding the Graphics Pipeline

The graphics pipeline is a fundamental concept in both OpenGL and WebGL. It represents the sequence of stages that a 3D scene goes through before appearing on the screen. Understanding the graphics pipeline is crucial for optimizing rendering performance, implementing advanced effects, and troubleshooting graphical issues.

Stages of the Graphics Pipeline

The graphics pipeline consists of several stages, each responsible for specific tasks. While the exact details may vary between OpenGL and WebGL, the core stages remain similar:

1. **Vertex Processing**: This stage begins with the vertex data provided by your application. Vertex shaders, written in GLSL, operate on this data and perform transformations, lighting calculations, and other operations on individual vertices. The output is a set of transformed vertices.
2. **Primitive Assembly**: After vertex processing, vertices are assembled into geometric primitives, such as points, lines, or triangles. The type of primitive depends on the rendering mode specified by your application.
3. **Rasterization**: Rasterization converts geometric primitives into fragments or pixels on the screen. It determines which fragments are within the view frustum and should be part of the final image. This stage calculates fragment positions

and attributes within the viewport.

4. **Fragment Processing**: Fragment shaders, also written in GLSL, operate on the fragments generated during rasterization. They determine the final color of each fragment based on various factors, including lighting, textures, and material properties.
5. **Per-Fragment Operations**: After fragment processing, per-fragment operations like depth testing, blending, and stencil testing are applied. These operations determine the final values for each fragment's color, depth, and other attributes.
6. **Framebuffer**: The final fragments are written to the framebuffer, which represents the screen or an off-screen rendering target. The contents of the framebuffer are what you ultimately see on the screen.

Parallel Processing

One key advantage of the graphics pipeline is its ability to perform many tasks in parallel. Modern GPUs consist of thousands of processing cores, allowing them to handle a massive number of vertices and fragments simultaneously. This parallelism is crucial for achieving real-time rendering in complex 3D scenes.

Programmability

The flexibility of the graphics pipeline is greatly enhanced by programmable shaders. Vertex and fragment shaders enable developers to customize the behavior of the pipeline stages. This programmability is what allows for advanced lighting models, complex materials, and realistic effects in 3D graphics.

Conclusion

Understanding the graphics pipeline is a fundamental aspect of graphics programming in both OpenGL and WebGL. Each stage plays a crucial role in the rendering process, and knowledge of how they work together is essential for optimizing performance and achieving the desired visual effects in your graphics applications. In the following sections of this chapter, we will delve deeper into the specifics of the OpenGL and WebGL pipelines, highlighting their differences and similarities.

Section 4.2: Stages of the OpenGL Pipeline

In this section, we'll take a closer look at the stages of the OpenGL graphics pipeline. Understanding these stages is essential for anyone working with OpenGL, as they provide insights into how 3D graphics are processed and rendered.

Vertex Processing Stage

The first stage of the OpenGL pipeline is the vertex processing stage. In this stage, vertex data is transformed by vertex shaders. Vertex shaders are small programs written in GLSL (OpenGL Shading Language) and are executed on the GPU for each vertex in the scene. Common operations in this stage include applying transformations (e.g., translation, rotation, scaling) and performing lighting calculations.

Here's a simplified example of a vertex shader in OpenGL:

```
#version 330 core

layout(location = 0) in vec3 inPosition; // Vertex position attribute
```

```
uniform mat4 modelViewProjectionMatrix; // Combined model-view-projection matrix

out vec4 fragColor; // Output color

void main() {

// Transform vertex position

gl_Position = modelViewProjectionMatrix * vec4(inPosition, 1.0);

// Set output color

fragColor = vec4(1.0, 0.0, 0.0, 1.0); // Red color

}
```

Primitive Assembly Stage

After the vertex processing stage, vertices are assembled into geometric primitives. These primitives can be points, lines, or triangles, depending on the rendering mode specified by the application. For example, if you're rendering a 3D model, triangles are commonly used as primitives.

Rasterization Stage

The rasterization stage is where geometric primitives are converted into fragments or pixels on the screen. It determines which fragments fall within the view frustum and should be included in the final image. Rasterization calculates fragment positions and attributes within the viewport.

Fragment Processing Stage

In the fragment processing stage, fragment shaders take center stage. Fragment shaders are also written in GLSL and are executed on the GPU for each fragment generated during rasterization. These shaders determine the final color of each fragment, incorporating lighting calculations, textures, and material properties.

Here's a simplified example of a fragment shader in OpenGL:

```
#version 330 core

in vec4 fragColor; // Input color

out vec4 outputColor; // Output color

void main() {

// Output the input color as is

outputColor = fragColor;

}
```

Per-Fragment Operations

After fragment processing, various per-fragment operations are applied. These operations include depth testing (to determine which fragments are visible), blending (combining fragments with the framebuffer contents), and stencil testing (used for complex rendering effects).

Framebuffer Stage

Finally, the resulting fragments are written to the framebuffer, which represents the screen or an off-screen rendering target. The contents of the framebuffer are what you ultimately see on the screen.

Understanding these stages of the OpenGL pipeline is crucial for optimizing rendering performance, implementing custom shaders, and achieving desired visual effects in 3D graphics applications. In the subsequent sections, we'll explore the stages of the WebGL pipeline, highlighting both similarities and differences with OpenGL.

Section 4.3: Stages of the WebGL Pipeline

In this section, we'll dive into the stages of the WebGL graphics pipeline. WebGL is based on OpenGL ES 2.0 and operates within the web browser, making it a powerful tool for creating 3D graphics and interactive experiences on the web. Understanding the WebGL pipeline is essential for web developers and graphics programmers working with this technology.

Vertex Processing Stage

The first stage of the WebGL pipeline is the vertex processing stage. It is similar to the corresponding stage in OpenGL. In this stage, vertex data is transformed by vertex shaders, which are written in GLSL (WebGL's shading language). Vertex shaders perform operations like transforming vertices, applying lighting calculations, and preparing data for subsequent stages.

Here's a simplified example of a vertex shader in WebGL:

attribute vec3 aPosition; *// Vertex position attribute*

uniform mat4 uModelViewProjectionMatrix; *// Combined model-view-projection matrix*

varying vec4 vFragColor; *// Varying variable to pass data to the fragment shader*

void main() {

// Transform vertex position

```
gl_Position = uModelViewProjectionMatrix * vec4(aPosition, 1.0);

// Pass data to the fragment shader

vFragColor = vec4(1.0, 0.0, 0.0, 1.0); // Red color

}
```

Primitive Assembly Stage

In WebGL, as in OpenGL, vertices are assembled into geometric primitives after the vertex processing stage. Common primitives include points, lines, and triangles, depending on the rendering mode specified by the application.

Rasterization Stage

WebGL's rasterization stage is responsible for converting geometric primitives into fragments or pixels on the screen. It determines which fragments are within the viewport and should be part of the final image. Rasterization calculates fragment positions and attributes.

Fragment Processing Stage

The fragment processing stage in WebGL is analogous to that in OpenGL. Fragment shaders, written in GLSL, operate on the fragments generated during rasterization. They determine the final color of each fragment based on lighting calculations, textures, and material properties.

Here's a simplified example of a fragment shader in WebGL:

```
precision mediump float; // Set the precision for floating-point calculations
```

```
varying vec4 vFragColor; // Input color from the vertex shader

void main() {

// Output the input color as is

gl_FragColor = vFragColor;

}
```

Per-Fragment Operations

WebGL also includes per-fragment operations, similar to OpenGL. These operations include depth testing, blending, and stencil testing, which determine the final values for each fragment's color, depth, and other attributes.

Framebuffer Stage

Finally, the resulting fragments are written to the framebuffer. This framebuffer represents either the screen or an off-screen rendering target. The contents of the framebuffer are what users see on their web browsers.

Understanding the stages of the WebGL pipeline is crucial for creating 3D graphics and interactive web applications. WebGL provides a powerful platform for graphics programming on the web, and mastering its pipeline stages is essential for building immersive and visually engaging experiences. In the following sections, we will explore the differences and similarities between the OpenGL and WebGL pipelines and delve into optimization techniques for both environments.

Section 4.4: Differences and Similarities in Pipelines

In this section, we'll compare the graphics pipelines of OpenGL and WebGL, highlighting their differences and similarities. Understanding these distinctions is essential for developers who work with both technologies or transition between them.

WebGL: A Subset of OpenGL

WebGL is based on OpenGL ES 2.0, which is a subset of the full OpenGL specification. This means that WebGL lacks some of the advanced features and functionality found in OpenGL. WebGL was designed to run within web browsers, and its limited feature set ensures compatibility and security within the web environment.

Shader Programming

Both OpenGL and WebGL rely on shader programming for customizing the rendering process. Vertex and fragment shaders are essential components of both pipelines. You write shaders in GLSL, a language that's consistent between OpenGL and WebGL. This similarity makes it easier for developers to transfer their shader programming skills between the two platforms.

Web-Specific Considerations

WebGL has unique considerations due to its web-based nature. One critical aspect is security. WebGL enforces strict security policies to prevent malicious code from accessing the user's GPU and potentially compromising system integrity. This security layer is not present in traditional OpenGL.

WebGL Context Creation

In WebGL, obtaining a rendering context is different from traditional OpenGL. You must request a WebGL context from an HTML <canvas> element. This context provides access to WebGL functions and resources. In contrast, OpenGL contexts are typically created directly using platform-specific APIs or libraries.

```
const canvas = document.getElementById('myCanvas');

const gl = canvas.getContext('webgl'); // Obtaining a WebGL context in the web environment
```

WebGL's Restricted Environment

WebGL operates in a more restricted environment compared to OpenGL. For example, file access, network communication, and direct interaction with hardware are limited in WebGL to ensure security and sandboxing within the browser. Traditional OpenGL applications do not have these restrictions.

WebGL's GLSL Version

WebGL primarily supports GLSL ES (OpenGL Shading Language for Embedded Systems), which is a simplified version of GLSL. WebGL 2.0 introduced support for GLSL ES 3.00, bringing some compatibility with modern OpenGL shaders. However, it's essential to be aware of the version differences when porting shaders between OpenGL and WebGL.

Performance Considerations

Both OpenGL and WebGL aim for high performance, but WebGL's performance can be influenced by the underlying web browser and hardware. Developers need to consider browser-specific optimizations and limitations, whereas OpenGL applications typically target specific hardware and drivers.

WebGL Extensions

WebGL provides extensions that allow access to advanced features and hardware capabilities when available. These extensions can be critical for achieving specific rendering effects but should be used with caution as they may not be supported on all platforms.

Conclusion

OpenGL and WebGL share many similarities in their graphics pipelines, thanks to their common use of shader programming and GLSL. However, their differences, such as WebGL's web-specific considerations, security model, and context creation process, make it essential for developers to adapt their skills and strategies when transitioning between these two graphics programming environments. Understanding these distinctions enables developers to make informed decisions and optimize their graphics applications effectively.

Section 4.5: Optimizing the Graphics Pipeline

Optimizing the graphics pipeline is a crucial aspect of graphics programming in both OpenGL and WebGL. Efficient rendering can significantly impact the performance and visual quality of your applications. In this section, we'll explore various optimization strategies that apply to both environments.

1. Batch Rendering

Reducing the number of draw calls is a fundamental optimization technique. Minimizing draw calls by batching objects with similar properties together can significantly improve performance. For example, rendering multiple objects that share the same shader and material in a single draw call reduces overhead.

2. Culling Techniques

Implementing view frustum culling and occlusion culling can prevent unnecessary rendering of objects that are not visible or are hidden by other objects. This optimization reduces the workload on the GPU and improves frame rates.

3. Level of Detail (LOD)

LOD techniques involve using simplified models or textures for distant objects. As objects move farther from the camera, lower-detail versions are used, reducing the number of vertices and texture memory required for rendering.

4. Texture Atlases

Texture atlases combine multiple textures into a single larger texture. This technique reduces texture binding overhead and can improve rendering performance, especially when rendering many objects with different textures.

5. Shader Optimization

Optimizing shaders is critical for achieving good rendering performance. This includes minimizing the number of shader instructions, avoiding unnecessary calculations, and optimizing data access patterns in shaders.

6. Buffer Objects

Using buffer objects like vertex buffer objects (VBOs) and index buffer objects (IBOs) efficiently manages vertex and index data. These objects can be stored on the GPU, reducing data transfer overhead and improving rendering performance.

7. GPU Profiling

Profiling your GPU-bound code helps identify performance bottlenecks. Tools like WebGL Inspector for WebGL or GPU performance analyzers for OpenGL can provide insights into GPU utilization and help pinpoint areas that need optimization.

8. Avoiding State Changes

Minimizing state changes, such as shader switches or texture bindings, can improve rendering performance. Group rendering operations by state to reduce the overhead of changing rendering states.

9. Deferred Rendering

In some scenarios, deferred rendering can be more efficient than traditional forward rendering, especially when dealing with complex scenes and multiple light sources. It involves rendering object attributes to intermediate buffers and then performing lighting calculations in a separate pass.

10. Use of WebGL Extensions

When applicable, leverage WebGL extensions to access advanced features and hardware capabilities. WebGL extensions can provide performance benefits but should be used judiciously, considering compatibility across different browsers.

11. Texture Compression

Compressing textures can reduce memory bandwidth usage and improve loading times. WebGL supports texture compression formats like DXT and ETC1, which can be advantageous for mobile and web applications.

12. Minimize Overdraw

Overdraw occurs when multiple objects cover the same screen pixels, leading to redundant fragment shader executions. Techniques like depth testing and depth pre-pass can help reduce overdraw and improve rendering efficiency.

13. GPU Instancing

Both OpenGL and WebGL support GPU instancing, which allows rendering multiple instances of the same object with a single draw call. This can be particularly useful when rendering large numbers of identical objects, such as particles or foliage.

Conclusion

Optimizing the graphics pipeline is an ongoing process that requires careful consideration of your application's specific requirements and target platforms. By implementing these optimization strategies and continuously profiling and testing your graphics code, you can achieve smooth and visually appealing graphics performance in both OpenGL and WebGL applications. Keep in mind that performance improvements may vary depending on the complexity of your scenes and the capabilities of the hardware and browser environment.

Chapter 5: Shaders: The Heart of Modern Graphics

Section 5.1: Introduction to Shaders

Shaders are at the core of modern graphics programming in both OpenGL and WebGL. They are small programs written in shading languages like GLSL (OpenGL Shading Language) and are executed on the GPU. Shaders play a pivotal role in controlling the appearance of 3D objects and achieving a wide range of visual effects. In this section, we'll provide an introduction to shaders and their significance in graphics programming.

What Are Shaders?

Shaders are programs that run on the GPU and are responsible for various aspects of rendering, including vertex processing, fragment processing, and more. They allow developers to control how objects in a 3D scene are displayed, how light interacts with surfaces, and how textures are applied.

Types of Shaders

There are two primary types of shaders in graphics programming:

1. **Vertex Shaders**: These shaders operate on each vertex of a 3D model. They are responsible for transforming vertices from object space to screen space. Vertex shaders are commonly used for tasks like applying transformations, lighting calculations, and skinning animations.
2. **Fragment Shaders**: Fragment shaders, also known as pixel shaders, operate on each fragment (or pixel) generated during rasterization. They determine the final color of each

fragment, taking into account lighting, textures, and material properties.

Shader Languages

Shaders are typically written in shading languages such as GLSL (for OpenGL and WebGL), HLSL (High-Level Shading Language for DirectX), and CG (C for Graphics). GLSL is the most commonly used shading language for OpenGL-based graphics programming, including WebGL.

Shader Compilation

Before shaders can be executed on the GPU, they must be compiled. Compilation is the process of translating human-readable shader code into a format that the GPU can understand and execute. Shader compilation occurs at runtime when your graphics application is initialized.

Here's a simplified example of a vertex shader in GLSL:

```
#version 330 core

layout(location = 0) in vec3 inPosition; // Vertex position attribute

uniform mat4 modelViewProjectionMatrix; // Combined model-view-projection matrix

void main() {

// Transform vertex position

gl_Position = modelViewProjectionMatrix * vec4(inPosition, 1.0);

}
```

And a simple fragment shader in GLSL:

```
#version 330 core

out vec4 fragColor; // Output color

void main() {

// Set the output color to red

fragColor = vec4(1.0, 0.0, 0.0, 1.0);

}
```

Shader Program

In both OpenGL and WebGL, shaders are not used individually but are linked together into a shader program. A shader program consists of at least a vertex shader and a fragment shader. The program represents a complete rendering pipeline.

Conclusion

Shaders are fundamental to modern graphics programming and play a vital role in creating realistic 3D scenes and visual effects. Understanding how to write, compile, and use shaders is essential for anyone working in the field of graphics programming, whether it's for game development, simulations, or web-based interactive experiences. In the following sections, we'll explore shader development in both OpenGL and WebGL, including writing, compiling, and integrating shaders into the graphics pipeline.

Section 5.2: Writing and Compiling Shaders in OpenGL

In this section, we'll dive into the process of writing and compiling shaders in OpenGL. Shaders are essential components of the graphics pipeline, and they determine how 3D objects are rendered and displayed on the screen. We'll explore the steps involved in creating shaders and integrating them into your OpenGL application.

Shader Source Code

Shaders are typically written in GLSL (OpenGL Shading Language), which is a C-like language designed for graphics programming. GLSL provides a structured way to define the behavior of vertex and fragment shaders.

Here's a simplified example of a vertex shader written in GLSL:

```
#version 330 core

layout(location = 0) in vec3 inPosition; // Vertex position attribute

uniform mat4 modelViewProjectionMatrix; // Combined model-view-projection matrix

void main() {

// Transform vertex position

gl_Position = modelViewProjectionMatrix * vec4(inPosition, 1.0);

}
```

And here's a simple fragment shader in GLSL:

```
#version 330 core

out vec4 fragColor; // Output color

void main() {

// Set the output color to red
```

```
fragColor = vec4(1.0, 0.0, 0.0, 1.0);
}
```

Shader Compilation

Before shaders can be used in your OpenGL application, they must be compiled into a format that the GPU can execute. Shader compilation is typically done at runtime when your application initializes.

Here's a basic outline of the steps involved in compiling a shader in OpenGL:

1. Create a shader object of the appropriate type (vertex shader or fragment shader) using glCreateShader.
2. Set the shader source code using glShaderSource.
3. Compile the shader using glCompileShader.
4. Check for compilation errors using glGetShaderiv and glGetShaderInfoLog.
5. Attach the compiled shader to a shader program using glAttachShader.
6. Link the shader program using glLinkProgram.
7. Use the shader program for rendering by calling glUseProgram.

Shader Errors and Debugging

Shader compilation errors can occur due to syntax errors or logical issues in your shader code. It's crucial to check for compilation errors and log any error messages for debugging purposes.

Shader Program

In OpenGL, shaders are not used in isolation but are linked together into a shader program. A shader program represents a complete rendering pipeline and consists of at least a vertex shader and a fragment shader. You can create and manage shader programs using OpenGL functions like glCreateProgram, glAttachShader, and glLinkProgram.

Conclusion

Writing and compiling shaders in OpenGL is a fundamental aspect of graphics programming. Shaders define how your 3D objects are rendered and allow for a wide range of visual effects. Understanding the GLSL shader language and the shader compilation process is essential for creating visually appealing graphics in OpenGL applications. In the following sections, we'll explore similar concepts in the context of WebGL, highlighting the commonalities and differences between the two environments.

Section 5.3: Writing and Compiling Shaders in WebGL

In this section, we'll delve into the process of writing and compiling shaders in WebGL. Shaders are a fundamental component of WebGL programming, responsible for controlling the rendering process and achieving various visual effects. We'll explore the steps involved in creating shaders and integrating them into your WebGL application.

Shader Source Code

WebGL shaders are also written in GLSL (OpenGL Shading Language), similar to OpenGL. GLSL provides a structured way to define the behavior of vertex and fragment shaders in the WebGL context.

Here's a simplified example of a vertex shader written in GLSL for WebGL:

```
precision mediump float; // Set the precision for floating-point calculations

attribute vec3 aPosition; // Vertex position attribute

uniform mat4 uModelViewProjectionMatrix; // Combined model-view-projection matrix

void main() {

// Transform vertex position

gl_Position = uModelViewProjectionMatrix * vec4(aPosition, 1.0);

}
```

And here's a simple fragment shader in GLSL for WebGL:

```
precision mediump float; // Set the precision for floating-point calculations

void main() {

// Set the output color to red

gl_FragColor = vec4(1.0, 0.0, 0.0, 1.0);

}
```

Shader Compilation

The process of compiling shaders in WebGL is conceptually similar to OpenGL. Here's an outline of the steps involved:

1. Create a shader object of the appropriate type (vertex shader or fragment shader) using gl.createShader.
2. Set the shader source code using gl.shaderSource.
3. Compile the shader using gl.compileShader.
4. Check for compilation errors using gl.getShaderParameter and gl.getShaderInfoLog.
5. Create a shader program using gl.createProgram.
6. Attach the compiled shader to the shader program using gl.attachShader.
7. Link the shader program using gl.linkProgram.
8. Use the shader program for rendering by calling gl.useProgram.

Shader Errors and Debugging

As in OpenGL, shader compilation errors can occur in WebGL due to syntax errors or logical issues in your shader code. It's crucial to check for compilation errors and log any error messages for debugging purposes.

Shader Program

In WebGL, shaders are also used within a shader program, which represents a complete rendering pipeline. A shader program typically consists of at least a vertex shader and a fragment shader. You can create and manage shader programs in WebGL using functions like gl.createProgram, gl.attachShader, and gl.linkProgram.

Conclusion

Writing and compiling shaders in WebGL is a fundamental skill for graphics programming on the web. Shaders control the rendering process and allow for a wide range of visual effects, just like in the OpenGL environment. Understanding the GLSL shader language and the shader compilation process is essential for creating interactive and visually appealing graphics in WebGL applications. In the following sections, we'll explore shader optimization techniques and cross-compilation between OpenGL and WebGL, highlighting best practices for efficient graphics programming.

Section 5.4: Shader Optimization Techniques

Optimizing shaders is a critical aspect of graphics programming in both OpenGL and WebGL. Well-optimized shaders can significantly improve rendering performance and allow for more complex visual effects. In this section, we'll explore various shader optimization techniques that apply to both environments.

1. Minimize Redundant Calculations

One of the key principles of shader optimization is to minimize redundant calculations. Avoid recalculating values that remain constant within a shader pass. For example, if a value is constant for all fragments in a shader, compute it once and reuse it.

```
// Example of minimizing redundant calculations

vec3 normal = normalize(vertexNormal);

float lightingFactor = dot(normal, lightDirection);
```

2. Reduce Texture Fetches

Texture fetches can be a significant bottleneck in shaders. Minimize the number of texture samples by using techniques like texture atlases or mipmapping. Additionally, consider using lower-resolution textures for objects that are distant from the camera.

```
// Example of mipmapping for texture sampling

vec4 texColor = texture2D(mipmappedTexture, textureCoordinates);
```

3. Optimize Loops

Avoid complex loops in shaders, especially nested loops. Unrolling loops can sometimes lead to better performance. Keep in mind that shader compilers may not always optimize loops effectively, so manual optimization may be necessary.

```
// Example of loop unrolling

for (int i = 0; i < 4; ++i) {

// Loop body

}
```

4. Use Approximations

In some cases, using approximations for calculations can lead to performance gains. For example, using fast inverse square root approximations instead of the costly sqrt function can improve performance.

```
// Example of a fast inverse square root approximation
```

```
float fastInverseSqrt(float x) {
float halfx = 0.5 * x;
int i = floatBitsToInt(x);
i = 0x5f3759df - (i >> 1);
x = intBitsToFloat(i);
x = x * (1.5 - halfx * x * x);
return x;
}
```

5. Conditional Branching

Be cautious with conditional branching in shaders. Branching can lead to divergent execution paths on the GPU, reducing parallelism and performance. Whenever possible, try to use conditional statements that affect fewer fragments.

```
// Example of conditional branching with care
if (condition) {
// Branch for some fragments
} else {
// Branch for other fragments
}
```

6. Precision

Choose the appropriate precision for your shader variables. Using higher precision (e.g., highp) when lower precision (e.g., mediump) is sufficient can impact performance. Carefully consider the trade-off between precision and performance.

```
// Example of specifying precision

precision mediump float;
```

7. Use Built-in Functions

Shader compilers often optimize built-in functions more efficiently than custom implementations. Whenever possible, rely on built-in functions for common operations like trigonometry or vector math.

```
// Example of using built-in functions

float cosineValue = cos(angle);
```

8. Profile and Benchmark

Profiling and benchmarking your shaders are essential steps in optimization. Use tools like the OpenGL Profiler (gDEBugger) or WebGL Inspector to identify performance bottlenecks and monitor GPU usage.

Conclusion

Shader optimization is a complex and iterative process that involves a deep understanding of shader programming and the target hardware. By applying these optimization techniques, you can achieve better performance and create visually impressive graphics in both OpenGL and WebGL applications. Keep in mind that optimization strategies may vary depending on the specific requirements of your graphics application and the capabilities of the underlying hardware.

Section 5.5: Cross-Compiling Shaders from OpenGL to WebGL

Cross-compiling shaders between OpenGL and WebGL can be a valuable technique when developing applications for both desktop and web platforms. While OpenGL and WebGL share the same GLSL shader language, there are differences and considerations to keep in mind when making shaders compatible with both environments. In this section, we'll explore the process of cross-compiling shaders and ensuring compatibility.

Common Shader Language

The shader language used in both OpenGL and WebGL is GLSL (OpenGL Shading Language). This common language makes it possible to write shaders that can be compiled and executed in both environments with minimal modification.

```
// Example of a simple GLSL shader code

#version 330 core

void main() {

// Shader code here

}
```

WebGL-Specific Considerations

When writing shaders for cross-compilation, it's essential to consider WebGL's limitations and specific requirements:

1. **Precision Specifiers**: WebGL requires precision specifiers (e.g., precision mediump float;) at the beginning of shader code for all float variables. OpenGL may not enforce this requirement but adding precision specifiers ensures compatibility.
2. **Texture Functions**: WebGL may not support some texture functions that are available in OpenGL. Check the WebGL specification and use only supported functions for texture sampling and manipulation.
3. **Extension Support**: WebGL shaders may require specific extensions to access certain features or hardware capabilities. Ensure that you check for and enable necessary extensions in your WebGL context.
4. **Error Handling**: WebGL requires a different approach to error handling compared to OpenGL. Use WebGL-specific functions like gl.getShaderInfoLog and gl.getProgramInfoLog to retrieve shader and program compilation/linking error messages.

Conditional Compilation

To handle WebGL-specific differences while cross-compiling shaders, you can use conditional compilation directives. These directives allow you to include or exclude sections of code based on the target environment.

// Example of conditional compilation for WebGL

#ifdef WEBGL

// WebGL-specific code here

#else

// OpenGL-specific code here

```
#endif
```

By defining a WEBGL macro in your WebGL application, you can use it as a flag to conditionally include or exclude specific shader code.

Testing and Validation

When cross-compiling shaders, rigorous testing is essential. Verify that shaders work correctly in both OpenGL and WebGL environments by running test cases and comparing the output. Pay close attention to visual discrepancies and performance differences.

Shader Minification

For WebGL applications, shader minification can be beneficial. Minification tools reduce shader code size by eliminating unnecessary whitespace and optimizing variable names. Smaller shader files can lead to faster loading times for web-based applications.

Conclusion

Cross-compiling shaders from OpenGL to WebGL and vice versa can streamline the development process and allow you to reach a broader audience with your graphics applications. By adhering to WebGL's specific requirements and using conditional compilation, you can maintain shader compatibility while taking advantage of both desktop and web platforms for your graphics projects. Remember to thoroughly test and validate shaders in both environments to ensure consistent and optimal performance.

Chapter 6: Textures and Lighting

Section 6.1: Basics of Texturing

Textures play a fundamental role in computer graphics by adding detail and realism to objects and scenes. In this section, we will explore the basics of texturing, including what textures are, how they are applied to objects, and the different types of textures commonly used in graphics programming.

What are Textures?

Textures are 2D or 3D images that are mapped onto the surfaces of 3D objects in a graphics scene. These images contain color information and can represent various surface attributes, such as color, reflectivity, roughness, and more. Textures are used to enhance the appearance of objects, making them look more detailed and realistic.

Texture Coordinates

To apply a texture to an object, we use texture coordinates. These coordinates specify how the texture is mapped onto the object's surface. Texture coordinates are typically defined in a 2D space, with values ranging from 0 to 1. The (0, 0) coordinate corresponds to the bottom-left corner of the texture, and (1, 1) corresponds to the top-right corner.

Texture Mapping

Texture mapping is the process of applying a texture to an object's surface based on its texture coordinates. When rendering a textured object, the graphics pipeline interpolates the texture coordinates for each fragment (pixel) and samples the texture to determine the color or other properties of that fragment.

Types of Textures

1. **Color Textures**: These textures contain color information and are used to add surface color and detail to objects. Color textures are often used for materials like wood, bricks, or fabrics.
2. **Normal Maps**: Normal maps store surface normals in an RGB format. They are used to simulate surface detail by altering how light interacts with the object's surface, creating the illusion of bumps and crevices.
3. **Bump Maps**: Similar to normal maps, bump maps encode surface height information. They affect the shading of an object but do not modify its silhouette.
4. **Specular Maps**: Specular maps control the shininess or reflectivity of an object's surface. They determine where highlights appear on the object.
5. **Alpha Maps**: Alpha maps store transparency information. They define which parts of the texture are opaque and which are transparent, allowing for complex shapes and cutouts.

Texture Filtering

Texture filtering determines how the texture is sampled when the texture coordinates do not align perfectly with texel (texture pixel) boundaries. Common filtering modes include nearest-neighbor (pixelated) and linear (smooth) filtering.

Wrapping Modes

Textures can also have different wrapping modes, which determine how texture coordinates outside the range [0, 1] are handled. Common wrapping modes include repeat, clamp, and mirror.

Understanding the basics of texturing is crucial for creating realistic and visually appealing graphics in both OpenGL and WebGL. In the following sections, we'll explore how to implement textures in OpenGL and WebGL, enabling you to add detailed and lifelike surfaces to your 3D models.

Section 6.2: Implementing Textures in OpenGL

In this section, we will delve into the process of implementing textures in OpenGL, a fundamental aspect of creating visually engaging 3D graphics. Textures are used to provide detailed surface appearances to objects in a scene, and understanding how to apply them is crucial for realistic rendering.

Texture Loading

Before we can apply textures to objects, we need to load texture images. These images can be in various formats like JPEG, PNG, or BMP. Libraries like SOIL (Simple OpenGL Image Library) and STB Image make texture loading straightforward in OpenGL.

Here's a basic example of loading a texture in OpenGL using the SOIL library:

```
GLuint textureID;

glGenTextures(1, &textureID);
```

```
glBindTexture(GL_TEXTURE_2D, textureID);

int width, height;

unsigned char* image = SOIL_load_image("texture.jpg", &width, &height, 0, SOIL_LOAD_RGB);

glTexImage2D(GL_TEXTURE_2D, 0, GL_RGB, width, height, 0, GL_RGB, GL_UNSIGNED_BYTE, image);

SOIL_free_image_data(image);

glGenerateMipmap(GL_TEXTURE_2D);

// Set texture parameters (optional)

glTexParameteri(GL_TEXTURE_2D, GL_TEXTURE_WRAP_S, GL_REPEAT);

glTexParameteri(GL_TEXTURE_2D, GL_TEXTURE_WRAP_T, GL_REPEAT);

glTexParameteri(GL_TEXTURE_2D, GL_TEXTURE_MIN_FILTER, GL_LINEAR_MIPMAP_LINEAR);

glTexParameteri(GL_TEXTURE_2D, GL_TEXTURE_MAG_FILTER, GL_LINEAR);
```

Binding Textures

In OpenGL, textures must be bound to texture units before they can be used in shaders. This allows multiple textures to be used simultaneously. Commonly, texture units 0, 1, 2, etc., are used for binding textures.

```
glActiveTexture(GL_TEXTURE0); // Activate texture unit 0
```

glBindTexture(GL_TEXTURE_2D, textureID); *// Bind the texture to unit 0*

Texture Coordinates

To map a texture to an object, you need to specify texture coordinates for each vertex of the object. These coordinates are typically provided as vertex attributes and interpolated across the object's surface during rendering.

Fragment Shader and Texture Sampling

In the fragment shader, you can sample the texture using the interpolated texture coordinates. The sampled color can then be used to color the fragment.

```
#version 330 core

in vec2 TexCoord; // Interpolated texture coordinates from vertex shader

out vec4 FragColor;

uniform sampler2D textureSampler; // Texture unit 0

void main() {

FragColor = texture(textureSampler, TexCoord);

}
```

Texture Wrapping and Filtering

OpenGL provides various options for texture wrapping and filtering, allowing you to control how textures behave when mapped to objects. Wrapping modes include GL_REPEAT,

GL_CLAMP_TO_EDGE, and GL_MIRRORED_REPEAT, while filtering modes include nearest-neighbor and linear filtering.

Mipmapping

Mipmapping is a technique that involves precomputing smaller versions (mipmaps) of a texture to improve rendering quality at different distances from the camera. It can be enabled using glGenerateMipmap and provides better texture quality during both close-up and distant rendering.

Anisotropic Filtering

Anisotropic filtering is another filtering technique that enhances texture quality, especially when textures are viewed at oblique angles. It can significantly improve texture clarity in certain scenarios and is available in modern OpenGL.

Implementing textures in OpenGL allows you to add surface details, colors, and realistic appearances to your 3D objects. Texture mapping is a critical component of computer graphics, and mastering it is essential for creating visually appealing and immersive 3D scenes. In the next sections, we will explore how to implement textures in the context of WebGL, bringing the world of web-based graphics to life.

Section 6.3: Implementing Textures in WebGL

In this section, we will explore how to implement textures in WebGL, the graphics language for the web. Textures are crucial for enhancing the visual quality of web-based 3D graphics, and understanding their implementation in WebGL is essential for creating immersive web experiences.

Texture Loading

Loading textures in WebGL typically involves loading image files, such as PNG or JPEG, and creating WebGL texture objects. You can use the Image class in JavaScript to load images and then bind them to WebGL textures.

```
const texture = gl.createTexture();

gl.bindTexture(gl.TEXTURE_2D, texture);

const image = new Image();

image.src = 'texture.jpg';

image.onload = function() {

gl.bindTexture(gl.TEXTURE_2D, texture);

gl.texImage2D(gl.TEXTURE_2D, 0, gl.RGBA, gl.RGBA, gl.UNSIGNED_BYTE, image);

gl.generateMipmap(gl.TEXTURE_2D);

};
```

Binding Textures

WebGL uses texture units to manage multiple textures simultaneously. Before using a texture in a shader, you must bind it to a texture unit.

```
const textureUnit = 0; // Texture unit 0

gl.activeTexture(gl.TEXTURE0 + textureUnit);

gl.bindTexture(gl.TEXTURE_2D, texture);
```

Texture Coordinates

Similar to OpenGL, WebGL requires texture coordinates to map textures to objects. These coordinates are typically provided as attributes for each vertex and are interpolated across the object's surface during rendering.

Fragment Shader and Texture Sampling

In the fragment shader, you can sample textures using the texture2D function. The sampled color can be used to color the fragment.

```
precision mediump float;

varying vec2 vTextureCoord; // Interpolated texture coordinates from vertex shader

uniform sampler2D uTexture; // Texture unit 0

void main() {

gl_FragColor = texture2D(uTexture, vTextureCoord);

}
```

Texture Wrapping and Filtering

WebGL provides various options for texture wrapping and filtering. Wrapping modes include gl.REPEAT, gl.CLAMP_TO_EDGE, and gl.MIRRORED_REPEAT, while filtering modes include nearest-neighbor and linear filtering.

```
gl.texParameteri(gl.TEXTURE_2D, gl.TEXTURE_WRAP_S, gl.REPEAT);

gl.texParameteri(gl.TEXTURE_2D, gl.TEXTURE_WRAP_T, gl.REPEAT);
```

```
gl.texParameteri(gl.TEXTURE_2D,
gl.TEXTURE_MIN_FILTER,
gl.LINEAR_MIPMAP_LINEAR);

gl.texParameteri(gl.TEXTURE_2D,
gl.TEXTURE_MAG_FILTER, gl.LINEAR);
```

Mipmapping

Mipmapping is supported in WebGL and can be enabled by generating mipmaps using gl.generateMipmap. Mipmapping improves texture quality at different viewing distances, providing smoother transitions.

Anisotropic Filtering

WebGL also supports anisotropic filtering, which can be enabled to improve texture clarity at oblique angles. This feature enhances the visual quality of textures, especially when they are viewed from acute angles.

Implementing textures in WebGL is essential for creating rich and visually appealing web-based 3D graphics. It allows you to add details, colors, and realistic appearances to your 3D models, enhancing the overall user experience. In the next sections, we will explore more advanced graphics techniques and how they can be applied in the context of WebGL.

Section 6.4: Lighting Models in Graphics Programming

Lighting is a critical component of realistic 3D graphics, and understanding lighting models is essential for creating visually appealing scenes. In this section, we will explore various lighting models commonly used in graphics programming, both in OpenGL and WebGL.

Phong Lighting Model

The Phong lighting model is a widely used model for simulating the interaction of light with surfaces. It consists of three main components:

1. **Ambient Light**: Ambient light represents the overall illumination of a scene. It is a constant color that is added to all objects in the scene, regardless of their orientation or position. Ambient light provides a baseline level of illumination.
2. **Diffuse Reflection**: Diffuse reflection accounts for the scattered light that is uniformly emitted in all directions by a rough surface. It depends on the angle between the surface normal and the direction of the incoming light. The Lambertian reflectance model is a common choice for diffuse reflection.
3. **Specular Reflection**: Specular reflection models the reflection of light in a specific direction, creating highlights on the surface. The Phong reflection model uses a specular exponent to control the size and intensity of the highlights. Higher values result in smaller, more intense highlights.

Blinn-Phong Lighting Model

The Blinn-Phong lighting model is a variation of the Phong model that offers improved performance while maintaining a similar level of realism. It replaces the specular exponent with a half-vector calculation, which is computationally less expensive.

Implementing Lighting in OpenGL

In OpenGL, implementing lighting models typically involves writing shaders that calculate the lighting contributions for each fragment. Here's a simplified example of a fragment shader that implements the Phong lighting model:

```
#version 330 core

in vec3 FragPos; // Fragment position in world coordinates

in vec3 Normal; // Normal vector

in vec2 TexCoords; // Texture coordinates

out vec4 FragColor;

uniform vec3 lightPos; // Light position in world coordinates

uniform vec3 viewPos; // Camera position in world coordinates

uniform sampler2D textureSampler; // Texture unit 0

void main() {

// Ambient light

float ambientStrength = 0.1;

vec3 ambient = ambientStrength * texture(textureSampler, TexCoords).rgb;

// Diffuse reflection

vec3 lightDir = normalize(lightPos - FragPos);

float diff = max(dot(Normal, lightDir), 0.0);

vec3 diffuse = diff * texture(textureSampler, TexCoords).rgb;
```

```
// Specular reflection

float specularStrength = 0.5;

vec3 viewDir = normalize(viewPos - FragPos);

vec3 halfwayDir = normalize(lightDir + viewDir);

float spec = pow(max(dot(Normal, halfwayDir), 0.0), 32);

vec3 specular = specularStrength * spec * vec3(1.0, 1.0, 1.0);

FragColor = vec4(ambient + diffuse + specular, 1.0);

}
```

Implementing Lighting in WebGL

In WebGL, lighting can also be implemented in shaders. Here's a simplified example of a fragment shader in WebGL that implements the Phong lighting model:

```
precision mediump float;

varying vec3 FragPos; // Fragment position in world coordinates

varying vec3 Normal; // Normal vector

varying vec2 TexCoords; // Texture coordinates

uniform vec3 lightPos; // Light position in world coordinates

uniform vec3 viewPos; // Camera position in world coordinates

uniform sampler2D uTexture; // Texture unit 0

void main() {

// Ambient light
```

```
float ambientStrength = 0.1;

vec3 ambient = ambientStrength * texture2D(uTexture, TexCoords).rgb;

// Diffuse reflection

vec3 lightDir = normalize(lightPos - FragPos);

float diff = max(dot(Normal, lightDir), 0.0);

vec3 diffuse = diff * texture2D(uTexture, TexCoords).rgb;

// Specular reflection

float specularStrength = 0.5;

vec3 viewDir = normalize(viewPos - FragPos);

vec3 halfwayDir = normalize(lightDir + viewDir);

float spec = pow(max(dot(Normal, halfwayDir), 0.0), 32.0);

vec3 specular = specularStrength * spec * vec3(1.0, 1.0, 1.0);

gl_FragColor = vec4(ambient + diffuse + specular, 1.0);

}
```

Understanding lighting models and their implementation in OpenGL and WebGL is crucial for creating realistic 3D scenes. By controlling the ambient, diffuse, and specular components, you can achieve a wide range of lighting effects, from subtle shading to shiny highlights, adding depth and realism to your graphics. In the following sections, we will explore techniques for simulating realistic lighting and shadows in both OpenGL and WebGL.

Section 6.5: Simulating Realistic Lighting and Shadows

Simulating realistic lighting and shadows is a fundamental aspect of creating immersive 3D graphics in both OpenGL and WebGL. Realistic lighting and shadows enhance the visual quality of scenes and contribute to a more convincing and immersive experience for users. In this section, we will explore techniques for achieving realistic lighting and shadows in graphics programming.

Shadow Mapping

Shadow mapping is a widely used technique for simulating shadows in 3D graphics. It works by rendering the scene from the perspective of the light source and storing depth information in a texture known as the shadow map. During the final rendering pass, each pixel's depth is compared to the depth stored in the shadow map to determine whether it is in shadow or illuminated.

Here's a simplified overview of the shadow mapping process:

1. **Shadow Map Generation**: Render the scene from the perspective of the light source, capturing depth information in a texture.
2. **Shadow Map Sampling**: During the final rendering pass, sample the shadow map to determine the depth at the current pixel's position.
3. **Shadow Test**: Compare the sampled depth to the depth of the current pixel. If the sampled depth is greater (farther) than the pixel's depth, it is in shadow; otherwise, it is illuminated.

Phong Shading with Shadows

To achieve realistic lighting and shadows in OpenGL and WebGL, you can extend the Phong shading model we discussed earlier. Here's how to incorporate shadows into the shader:

```
#version 330 core

in vec3 FragPos; // Fragment position in world coordinates

in vec3 Normal; // Normal vector

in vec2 TexCoords; // Texture coordinates

out vec4 FragColor;

uniform vec3 lightPos; // Light position in world coordinates

uniform vec3 viewPos; // Camera position in world coordinates

uniform sampler2D textureSampler; // Texture unit 0

uniform sampler2D shadowMap; // Texture unit 1 (shadow map)

void main() {

// Calculate shadow factor

vec3 fragToLight = lightPos - FragPos;

vec3 projCoords = FragPos;

projCoords.z -= 0.005; // Bias to avoid self-shadowing artifacts

float depth = texture(shadowMap, projCoords.xy).r;

float shadowFactor = (projCoords.z > depth + 0.005) ? 1.0 : 0.5; // Adjust bias value as needed
```

```
// Ambient light, diffuse reflection, and specular reflection as before

FragColor = vec4((ambient + (shadowFactor * diffuse) + specular) * texture(textureSampler, TexCoords).rgb, 1.0);

}
```

Cascaded Shadow Mapping

Cascaded Shadow Mapping (CSM) is an advanced technique that improves shadow quality in scenes with large depth ranges. It divides the view frustum into multiple "cascades," each with its own shadow map. This approach ensures that objects near the camera have higher shadow map resolutions, reducing shadow aliasing artifacts.

Soft Shadows

To achieve soft shadows, you can use techniques like Percentage Closer Soft Shadows (PCSS) or Variance Shadow Mapping (VSM). These methods introduce softness and penumbra to shadow edges, enhancing realism.

Simulating realistic lighting and shadows is a complex but rewarding aspect of 3D graphics programming. By incorporating shadow mapping and shading techniques into your OpenGL and WebGL applications, you can create visually compelling scenes with convincing lighting and shadows. In the following chapters, we will explore more advanced rendering techniques and optimizations to further enhance the quality of your graphics.

Chapter 7: 3D Models and Transformations

Section 7.1: Fundamentals of 3D Modeling

In the world of graphics programming, 3D modeling is at the core of creating complex and visually engaging scenes. It involves representing three-dimensional objects and scenes in a digital format that can be rendered on a 2D screen. In this section, we will delve into the fundamentals of 3D modeling, exploring the concepts and techniques essential for working with 3D objects in both OpenGL and WebGL.

Geometric Primitives

At the heart of 3D modeling are geometric primitives, which serve as the building blocks for creating 3D objects. These primitives include:

- **Points**: Represent a single point in space.
- **Lines**: Connect two points and can be used to define edges of shapes.
- **Triangles**: Composed of three vertices and are fundamental for rendering surfaces.
- **Quadrilaterals**: Composed of four vertices and are used for more complex surfaces.
- **Polygons**: Generalized shapes with three or more vertices.

Vertex Data

To create 3D models, you need to define the geometry of the objects using vertex data. Vertex data includes information about the position of each vertex in 3D space, as well as attributes like normals, texture coordinates, and colors. This data is organized into buffers that can be sent to the graphics card for rendering.

Meshes

A mesh is a collection of vertices and indices that define a 3D object's geometry. Meshes are the primary representation of 3D objects in graphics programming. They can be simple, like a single triangle, or highly complex, such as a detailed character model.

Transformations

Transformations are essential for positioning, scaling, and rotating 3D objects within a scene. Common transformations include:

- **Translation**: Moving an object in 3D space.
- **Rotation**: Changing an object's orientation.
- **Scaling**: Adjusting the size of an object.

Transformations are typically represented as matrices and applied to the vertex data of a mesh to position and orient it correctly.

Coordinate Systems

Understanding coordinate systems is crucial when working with 3D models. Common coordinate systems include:

- **World Coordinates**: The global coordinate system that defines the positions of objects in the world.

- **Local Coordinates**: The object's own coordinate system, which may differ from the world coordinates.
- **View Coordinates**: The coordinate system of the camera or viewer, used for rendering.
- **Normalized Device Coordinates (NDC)**: A standardized coordinate system where values range from -1 to 1 in each dimension.

Model-View-Projection (MVP) Matrix

The MVP matrix is a critical concept in 3D graphics. It combines three matrices: the model matrix (for object transformations), the view matrix (for camera position and orientation), and the projection matrix (for perspective or orthographic projection). Multiplying the vertex positions by the MVP matrix ultimately maps 3D objects to the 2D screen.

Loading 3D Models

In practice, 3D models are often created using specialized software such as Blender or Maya. These models can then be exported in common formats like OBJ or FBX and loaded into OpenGL or WebGL applications for rendering. Libraries and frameworks are available to simplify the process of loading and working with 3D models.

Understanding the fundamentals of 3D modeling, including geometric primitives, vertex data, transformations, and coordinate systems, lays the foundation for creating complex 3D scenes in OpenGL and WebGL. In the following sections, we will explore how to apply these concepts to work with 3D models, including loading, rendering, and manipulating them in a graphics programming context.

Section 7.2: Transformations in OpenGL and WebGL

Transformations play a pivotal role in positioning, orienting, and scaling 3D objects within a scene. In both OpenGL and WebGL, transformations are achieved through matrices, which are mathematical constructs used to represent various transformations. In this section, we will explore how transformations are implemented in OpenGL and WebGL and how they affect the rendering of 3D objects.

Model Matrix

The model matrix represents the transformations applied to an individual 3D object. These transformations include translation (moving the object), rotation (changing its orientation), and scaling (adjusting its size). In OpenGL and WebGL, you can construct the model matrix using libraries like GLM (OpenGL Mathematics) or manually using matrix operations.

Here's an example of how a model matrix is constructed in OpenGL using GLM:

```
glm::mat4 model = glm::mat4(1.0f); // Initialize as identity matrix

model = glm::translate(model, glm::vec3(2.0f, 1.0f, -3.0f)); // Translation

model = glm::rotate(model, glm::radians(45.0f), glm::vec3(0.0f, 1.0f, 0.0f)); // Rotation

model = glm::scale(model, glm::vec3(0.5f, 0.5f, 0.5f)); // Scaling
```

View Matrix

The view matrix defines the position and orientation of the camera or viewer within the 3D world. It effectively "moves" the entire world to simulate the camera's perspective. The view matrix is responsible for determining what is visible in the scene.

```
glm::mat4 view = glm::lookAt(
glm::vec3(0.0f, 0.0f, 3.0f), // Camera position
glm::vec3(0.0f, 0.0f, 0.0f), // Camera target
glm::vec3(0.0f, 1.0f, 0.0f) // Up vector
);
```

Projection Matrix

The projection matrix handles the mapping of 3D coordinates to 2D screen coordinates. It defines the type of projection, such as perspective or orthographic, and the field of view, aspect ratio, and near/far clipping planes.

For a perspective projection in OpenGL:

```
glm::mat4 projection = glm::perspective(
glm::radians(45.0f), // Field of view
800.0f / 600.0f, // Aspect ratio
0.1f, // Near clipping plane
100.0f // Far clipping plane
);
```

Model-View-Projection (MVP) Matrix

The MVP matrix combines the model, view, and projection matrices into a single matrix that is applied to the vertex positions of 3D objects during rendering. It transforms the object from its local space to world space, applies the camera's view, and projects it onto the 2D screen.

```
glm::mat4 mvp = projection * view * model;
```

Order of Transformations

The order in which transformations are applied matters. For example, changing the order of rotation and translation will produce different results. In OpenGL and WebGL, transformations are typically applied in the order: model, view, projection (MVP).

Understanding transformations and how to construct and apply matrices is fundamental when working with 3D objects in OpenGL and WebGL. These matrices allow you to control the position, orientation, and projection of objects within a 3D scene, providing the flexibility to create complex and visually engaging graphics. In the subsequent sections, we will explore further techniques and considerations for working with 3D models and their transformations.

Section 7.3: Transformations in WebGL

Transformations are a fundamental aspect of 3D graphics programming, allowing you to position, rotate, and scale 3D objects within a WebGL scene. In this section, we will explore how transformations are implemented in WebGL and how they impact the rendering of 3D objects.

Model Matrix

The model matrix represents the transformations applied to an individual 3D object. These transformations include translation (changing the object's position), rotation (altering its orientation), and scaling (adjusting its size). In WebGL, you can construct the model matrix using JavaScript.

Here's an example of how a model matrix can be constructed in WebGL:

```
const modelMatrix = mat4.create(); // Initialize as an identity matrix

mat4.translate(modelMatrix, modelMatrix, [2.0, 1.0, -3.0]); // Translation

mat4.rotate(modelMatrix, modelMatrix, Math.PI / 4, [0, 1, 0]); // Rotation

mat4.scale(modelMatrix, modelMatrix, [0.5, 0.5, 0.5]); // Scaling
```

View Matrix

The view matrix defines the position and orientation of the camera or viewer within the 3D world. It effectively simulates the camera's perspective by transforming the entire world. The view matrix is responsible for determining what is visible in the scene.

Here's an example of how a view matrix can be created in WebGL:

```
const viewMatrix = mat4.create();

mat4.lookAt(viewMatrix, [0, 0, 3], [0, 0, 0], [0, 1, 0]); // Define camera position, target, and up vector
```

Projection Matrix

The projection matrix handles the mapping of 3D coordinates to 2D screen coordinates. It defines the type of projection, such as perspective or orthographic, and includes parameters like field of view, aspect ratio, and near/far clipping planes.

For a perspective projection in WebGL:

```
const projectionMatrix = mat4.create();

mat4.perspective(projectionMatrix, Math.PI / 4, canvas.width / canvas.height, 0.1, 100.0); // Define perspective projection
```

Model-View-Projection (MVP) Matrix

The MVP matrix combines the model, view, and projection matrices into a single matrix that is applied to the vertex positions of 3D objects during rendering. It transforms the object from its local space to world space, applies the camera's view, and projects it onto the 2D screen.

```
const mvpMatrix = mat4.create();

mat4.multiply(mvpMatrix, projectionMatrix, viewMatrix); // Combine projection and view

mat4.multiply(mvpMatrix, mvpMatrix, modelMatrix); // Combine with model
```

Order of Transformations

The order in which transformations are applied is crucial. Changing the order of rotation and translation, for example, will produce different results. In WebGL, transformations are typically applied in the order: model, view, projection (MVP).

Understanding transformations and how to construct and apply matrices is fundamental when working with 3D objects in WebGL. These matrices allow you to control the position, orientation, and projection of objects within a 3D scene, providing the flexibility to create complex and visually engaging graphics. In the following sections, we will explore further techniques and considerations for working with 3D models and their transformations in WebGL.

Section 7.4: Importing and Rendering 3D Models

Rendering basic geometric shapes is essential in graphics programming, but real-world 3D applications often require more complex and detailed objects. In this section, we will explore how to import and render 3D models in WebGL, allowing you to incorporate intricate objects into your 3D scenes.

3D Model Formats

To render 3D models, you need a format to store and describe the geometry, materials, and other properties of the object. Common 3D model formats include Wavefront OBJ, Collada (DAE), and glTF (GL Transmission Format). These formats provide a structured way to represent 3D assets and are supported by various modeling software and libraries.

Loading 3D Models

To use a 3D model in WebGL, you first need to load it into your application. This involves reading the model file (e.g., OBJ or glTF) and extracting relevant information such as vertex positions, normals, texture coordinates, and material properties.

Here's a simplified example of loading a 3D model in WebGL using the glTF format:

```
// Initialize the glTF loader

const loader = new THREE.GLTFLoader();

// Load a glTF model

loader.load('model.gltf', (gltf) => {

const model = gltf.scene;

// Add the model to the scene

scene.add(model);

});
```

Rendering 3D Models

Once the 3D model is loaded, you can render it within your WebGL scene. This typically involves applying transformations, materials, and lighting as needed.

```
// Apply transformations

model.position.set(0, 0, 0);

model.rotation.set(0, Math.PI, 0);

model.scale.set(1, 1, 1);

// Define and apply materials (e.g., textures)

const material = new THREE.MeshStandardMaterial({ color: 0xffffff});

model.traverse((child) => {
```

```
if (child.isMesh) {
child.material = material;
}
});
```

Optimizing 3D Models

Imported 3D models may contain a high level of detail, which can impact performance. To optimize rendering, you can employ techniques like level-of-detail (LOD) rendering, culling, and mesh simplification. These methods help maintain good performance while preserving visual quality.

Interactivity with 3D Models

In interactive applications, you may want to allow users to interact with 3D models. This can involve picking (selecting) objects, applying transformations through user input, or triggering animations. WebGL provides the capability to handle user interactions and respond to events like mouse clicks or touch gestures.

Conclusion

Importing and rendering 3D models in WebGL opens up a world of possibilities for creating rich and immersive 3D environments. Whether you're building games, simulations, or interactive web applications, the ability to work with external 3D assets enhances the realism and complexity of your projects. In the next section, we will explore techniques for managing complex transformations and animations of 3D models within your WebGL scenes.

Section 7.5: Managing Complex Transformations

In WebGL, creating complex 3D scenes often involves managing multiple 3D objects, each with its own transformations and animations. This section delves into techniques for efficiently handling complex transformations, orchestrating animations, and managing the scene graph in WebGL applications.

Scene Graph

A scene graph is a hierarchical representation of the objects in a 3D scene. It allows you to organize and control transformations for different objects in relation to each other. The root of the scene graph represents the entire scene, and child nodes can be added to represent objects or parts of objects.

Here's an example of creating a simple scene graph in WebGL using the Three.js library:

```
const scene = new THREE.Scene();

const object1 = new THREE.Mesh(geometry1, material1);

const object2 = new THREE.Mesh(geometry2, material2);

scene.add(object1); // object1 is a child of the scene

object1.add(object2); // object2 is a child of object1
```

Hierarchical Transformations

The hierarchical structure of a scene graph allows you to apply transformations hierarchically. When you transform a parent node, all its children inherit the transformation. This feature is especially useful for animating complex objects composed of multiple parts.

```
// Rotate the parent object
object1.rotation.y += 0.01;
// The child object inherits the rotation
object2.rotation.y += 0.02;
```

Animation Sequences

Complex animations often involve a sequence of transformations over time. You can use keyframe animations to specify how objects change their positions, rotations, and scales over a duration.

Here's a simplified example of keyframe animation in Three.js:

```
const keyframes = [
{ position: { x: 0, y: 0, z: 0 }, rotation: { x: 0, y: 0, z: 0 } },
{ position: { x: 1, y: 2, z: 1 }, rotation: { x: Math.PI / 2, y: 0, z: 0 } },
// Add more keyframes as needed
];
const mixer = new THREE.AnimationMixer(object1);
const clip = THREE.AnimationClip.CreateFromKeyframeTrack(keyframes);
mixer.clipAction(clip).play();
```

Skinning and Morph Targets

For character animations and deformable objects, techniques like skinning and morph targets are used. Skinning involves attaching a mesh to a skeleton, allowing for realistic character animations.

Morph targets, on the other hand, deform a mesh's vertices to create various shapes or facial expressions.

Implementing skinning and morph targets can be complex, but they provide the foundation for lifelike character animations.

Performance Considerations

Managing complex transformations and animations can be computationally expensive. To maintain good performance, you should consider techniques like level-of-detail (LOD) rendering, culling, and GPU instancing. These optimizations help ensure that your WebGL application runs smoothly, even with intricate scenes.

Conclusion

Handling complex transformations and animations is a crucial aspect of WebGL development, particularly for applications that require realistic 3D scenes and character animations. Understanding how to organize your scene graph, apply hierarchical transformations, and create animations allows you to bring your 3D worlds to life. In the following chapters, we will explore further optimization strategies and delve into advanced rendering techniques to enhance the visual quality of your WebGL projects.

Chapter 8: User Interaction and Animation

Section 8.1: Capturing User Input

User interaction is a fundamental aspect of many WebGL applications. It enables users to navigate and interact with 3D scenes, control animations, and make choices in interactive applications. In this section, we will explore how to capture user input in WebGL, allowing you to create engaging and interactive experiences.

Mouse and Touch Events

Capturing mouse and touch events is a common way to enable user interaction. WebGL applications can respond to events like clicks, double-clicks, mouse movement, and touch gestures. Libraries like Three.js simplify event handling and provide abstractions for mouse and touch interactions.

Here's a basic example of handling a click event in Three.js:

```
// Add a click event listener to the renderer's DOM element

renderer.domElement.addEventListener('click', (event) => {

// Calculate the mouse position relative to the canvas

const mouse = new THREE.Vector2();

mouse.x = (event.clientX / window.innerWidth) * 2 - 1;

mouse.y = -(event.clientY / window.innerHeight) * 2 + 1;

// Perform raycasting to determine what the user clicked on
```

```
const raycaster = new THREE.Raycaster();

raycaster.setFromCamera(mouse, camera);

const intersects = raycaster.intersectObjects(scene.children, true);

if (intersects.length > 0) {

// An object was clicked, perform desired actions

const clickedObject = intersects[0].object;

console.log('Clicked object:', clickedObject);

}

});
```

Keyboard Input

Keyboard input is another way to capture user actions. You can listen for keydown and keyup events to handle keyboard input. This is useful for creating games, simulations, or applications that require keyboard control.

```
// Add a keydown event listener to the document

document.addEventListener('keydown', (event) => {

// Check the keycode to identify the pressed key

if (event.key === 'ArrowUp') {

// Perform an action, e.g., move the character forward

character.moveForward();

} else if (event.key === 'ArrowDown') {
```

```
// Perform an action, e.g., move the character backward
character.moveBackward();
}
});
```

Gamepad and VR Controllers

For more immersive experiences, you can integrate gamepad or virtual reality (VR) controller input. WebGL applications can utilize WebXR or other VR libraries to interact with VR headsets and controllers. This enables users to reach into the virtual world and manipulate objects or navigate environments.

```
// Example of handling WebXR controller input
const controller = renderer.xr.getController(0);
controller.addEventListener('squeezestart', (event) => {
// React to controller squeeze input
const targetObject = event.target;
console.log('Controller squeeze started on', targetObject);
});
```

Touchscreen Gestures

On touchscreen devices, you can implement gestures like pinch-to-zoom, swipe, or two-finger rotation. Libraries such as Hammer.js can simplify gesture recognition and handling in WebGL applications.

Conclusion

Capturing user input in WebGL opens up a world of possibilities for creating interactive and engaging 3D applications. Whether you're building games, simulations, data visualizations, or educational experiences, understanding how to capture and respond to user input is essential. In the following sections, we will explore how to implement interactive controls in both OpenGL and WebGL, enabling users to interact seamlessly with your 3D worlds.

Section 8.2: Implementing Interactive Controls in OpenGL

Implementing interactive controls in an OpenGL application is essential for user engagement and interaction with 3D graphics. In this section, we will explore various techniques and libraries that help you implement interactive controls in your OpenGL-based projects.

1. Handling Mouse Input

Handling mouse input is a fundamental part of creating interactive controls in OpenGL. You can use the GLFW library to capture mouse events such as mouse movement, button presses, and scrolling.

Here's a simple example of setting up mouse input in an OpenGL application using GLFW:

```
// Initialize GLFW and create a window

glfwInit();

GLFWwindow* window = glfwCreateWindow(800, 600, "OpenGL App", NULL, NULL);
```

```
glfwMakeContextCurrent(window);

// Set up mouse input callbacks

glfwSetCursorPosCallback(window, mouse_callback);

glfwSetScrollCallback(window, scroll_callback);

glfwSetMouseButtonCallback(window, mouse_button_callback);

while (!glfwWindowShouldClose(window)) {

// Main rendering loop

// ...

glfwSwapBuffers(window);

glfwPollEvents();

}

glfwTerminate();
```

2. Handling Keyboard Input

Keyboard input is essential for controlling objects or characters in an OpenGL application. GLFW also provides functions to capture keyboard input events.

Here's a basic example of handling keyboard input:

```
// Set up keyboard input callbacks

glfwSetKeyCallback(window, key_callback);

// Keyboard input callback function
```

```
void key_callback(GLFWwindow* window, int key, int scancode, int action, int mods) {

if (key == GLFW_KEY_W && action == GLFW_PRESS) {

// Handle key press (e.g., move forward)

}

// Other key handling logic

}
```

3. Implementing Camera Controls

In OpenGL applications, camera controls allow users to navigate the 3D scene. You can implement camera movement using user input from the keyboard and mouse. Libraries like GLM (OpenGL Mathematics) are helpful for managing camera transformations.

4. GUI Libraries

Integrating graphical user interface (GUI) libraries like ImGui can simplify the creation of interactive tools and settings panels in your OpenGL applications. ImGui provides an easy way to create buttons, sliders, and text input fields within your 3D scene.

5. Picking and Selection

Picking is a technique used to select objects in a 3D scene using the mouse cursor. It involves rendering the scene from the perspective of the camera and identifying which object is under the mouse cursor. This is useful for interacting with objects in the scene.

6. Third-Party Libraries

Several third-party libraries, such as Dear ImGui, SDL (Simple DirectMedia Layer), and SFML (Simple and Fast Multimedia Library), offer built-in support for user input handling and GUI creation in OpenGL applications.

7. Custom Controls

For more advanced interactive controls, you can create custom GUI elements and interaction systems tailored to your application's requirements. This may involve creating 3D widgets, sliders, or interactive objects within your scene.

Conclusion

Implementing interactive controls in OpenGL applications is essential for creating engaging and user-friendly 3D experiences. Whether you're building games, simulations, or data visualization tools, understanding how to handle mouse and keyboard input, manage camera controls, and integrate GUI libraries can greatly enhance user interaction. In the next section, we will explore how to implement interactive controls in WebGL, bringing similar interactive capabilities to web-based 3D applications.

Section 8.3: Implementing Interactive Controls in WebGL

In WebGL, implementing interactive controls is crucial for creating immersive and user-friendly 3D web applications. This section explores various techniques and libraries for implementing interactive controls in your WebGL-based projects.

1. Handling Mouse Input

Capturing mouse input is a fundamental aspect of enabling user interaction in WebGL. You can utilize JavaScript event listeners to capture mouse events such as clicks, movement, and scrolling.

Here's a basic example of handling mouse input in a WebGL application:

```
// Add a click event listener to the canvas element

canvas.addEventListener('click', (event) => {

// Calculate the mouse position relative to the canvas

const rect = canvas.getBoundingClientRect();

const x = event.clientX - rect.left;

const y = event.clientY - rect.top;

// Perform actions based on the mouse click position

console.log('Mouse clicked at (x:', x, ', y:', y, ')');

});
```

2. Handling Keyboard Input

Keyboard input is essential for controlling objects, characters, or camera movement in WebGL applications. You can use JavaScript event listeners to capture keyboard events like keydown and keyup.

```
// Add a keydown event listener to the document

document.addEventListener('keydown', (event) => {

// Check the keycode to identify the pressed key
```

```
if (event.key === 'ArrowUp') {
// Perform an action, e.g., move forward
} else if (event.key === 'ArrowDown') {
// Perform an action, e.g., move backward
}
});
```

3. Implementing Camera Controls

Camera controls allow users to navigate the 3D scene in WebGL applications. Libraries like Three.js provide built-in camera controls, making it easy to implement features like orbiting, panning, and zooming.

```
// Initialize a Three.js perspective camera with orbit controls
const camera = new THREE.PerspectiveCamera(75, window.innerWidth / window.innerHeight, 0.1, 1000);
const controls = new THREE.OrbitControls(camera, renderer.domElement);
// Update the controls in the render loop
function animate() {
requestAnimationFrame(animate);
controls.update();
renderer.render(scene, camera);
}
```

```
animate();
```

4. GUI Libraries

Integrating graphical user interface (GUI) libraries like dat.GUI or the built-in GUI system in Three.js can simplify the creation of interactive settings panels within your WebGL applications. These libraries allow you to create sliders, checkboxes, and buttons for controlling parameters in real-time.

5. Picking and Selection

Picking in WebGL involves determining which object in the 3D scene is under the mouse cursor when a user clicks. This technique is valuable for interacting with objects in the scene. Libraries like Three.js provide raycasting functionality for accurate picking.

6. Virtual Reality (VR) Controllers

For WebVR or WebXR applications, you can implement VR controller support to enable users to interact with 3D environments using VR controllers. This opens up possibilities for immersive VR experiences.

7. Custom Controls

To implement unique and specialized interactive controls, you can create custom interaction systems tailored to your WebGL application's requirements. This may involve creating 3D widgets, interactive objects, or innovative control mechanisms.

Conclusion

Implementing interactive controls in WebGL is essential for creating engaging and user-friendly 3D web applications. Whether you're building games, simulations, data visualizations, or educational experiences, understanding how to capture and respond to user input, manage camera controls, and integrate GUI libraries can greatly enhance user interaction. In the following section, we will explore the basics of animation in graphics programming, allowing you to create dynamic and responsive WebGL experiences.

Section 8.4: Basics of Animation in Graphics

Animation plays a significant role in graphics programming, enhancing the visual appeal and interactivity of 3D scenes. In this section, we will explore the fundamentals of animation in the context of OpenGL and WebGL.

Animation Concepts

1. **Frame Rate**: Animation in graphics programming relies on the concept of a frame rate, which determines how many frames (images) are displayed per second. Common frame rates are 24, 30, 60, or even higher. The frame rate affects the smoothness of animation.
2. **Keyframes**: Keyframes are specific frames in an animation sequence where important changes occur. By defining keyframes, you can interpolate between them to create fluid animations. Keyframes often represent the start and end points of a motion or transformation.

Animation Techniques

1. **Linear Interpolation (LERP)**: Linear interpolation is a straightforward technique to animate objects between keyframes. It involves calculating intermediate positions or values based on a linear progression between two

keyframes. LERP is suitable for simple linear motions.

2. **Easing Functions**: Easing functions add realism to animations by controlling the acceleration and deceleration of an object's movement. Common easing functions include ease-in, ease-out, and ease-in-out, each affecting the timing of animation differently.
3. **Skeletal Animation**: In 3D graphics, skeletal animation is used to animate characters and creatures. It involves defining a skeleton with bones and joints and then attaching the 3D model to the skeleton. By manipulating the bone transformations, you can achieve complex character animations.
4. **Blend Trees**: Blend trees are used in game development to combine multiple animations seamlessly. For example, a character can smoothly transition from walking to running by blending the animations together based on user input.
5. **Particle Systems**: Particle systems are essential for animating effects like fire, smoke, rain, and explosions. They simulate the behavior of thousands of individual particles, each following predefined rules, to create visually appealing effects.

Animation in OpenGL

In OpenGL, animation is achieved by updating the position, rotation, or other properties of objects in the scene over time. This typically involves recalculating the model-view matrix for each frame to animate objects.

Here's a simplified example of how you might perform animation in OpenGL:

// Define initial position and velocity

```
glm::vec3 position(0.0f, 0.0f, 0.0f);

glm::vec3 velocity(0.1f, 0.0f, 0.0f);

// Animation loop

while (!glfwWindowShouldClose(window)) {

// Calculate the new position based on velocity

position += velocity * deltaTime; // deltaTime is the time since the last frame

// Update the model-view matrix with the new position

glm::mat4 model = glm::translate(glm::mat4(1.0f), position);

// Render the object with the updated model-view matrix

// ...

// Swap buffers and poll events

// ...

}
```

Animation in WebGL

In WebGL, animation is typically accomplished using JavaScript. You can use the requestAnimationFrame function to create a loop that updates and renders your scene at a consistent frame rate.

Here's a simplified example of animation in WebGL:

```
// Animation loop using requestAnimationFrame

function animate() {
```

```
requestAnimationFrame(animate);
// Update object properties for the current frame
// ...
// Render the scene
render();
// Handle user input
// ...
}
// Start the animation loop
animate();
```

Conclusion

Animation is a vital component of graphics programming, allowing you to bring 3D scenes and objects to life. Whether you're creating simple linear animations or complex character movements, understanding animation concepts and techniques is crucial. In the next section, we will explore how to create smooth animations in both OpenGL and WebGL environments, ensuring a captivating user experience.

Section 8.5: Creating Smooth Animations in Both Environments

Creating smooth animations is essential to providing an engaging user experience in both OpenGL and WebGL environments. In this section, we'll discuss strategies and best practices for achieving fluid animations in your graphics applications.

Timing and Delta Time

One of the fundamental aspects of smooth animations is maintaining a consistent frame rate. In OpenGL and WebGL, this is typically achieved by using a timing mechanism that ensures your animations run at a fixed frame rate, such as 60 frames per second (FPS). The requestAnimationFrame function in WebGL and timing libraries in OpenGL can help you achieve this.

Delta time (often denoted as deltaTime) is the time elapsed since the last frame was rendered. It's crucial for achieving frame rate independence in animations. By multiplying your animation updates and movements by deltaTime, you ensure that the animation's speed remains consistent, regardless of the frame rate. Here's a simplified example in JavaScript:

```
let lastFrameTime = 0;

function animate(currentTime) {

requestAnimationFrame(animate);

// Calculate deltaTime

const deltaTime = (currentTime - lastFrameTime) / 1000; // Convert to seconds

// Update animations using deltaTime

updateAnimations(deltaTime);

// Render the scene

render();
```

```
lastFrameTime = currentTime;

}

// Start the animation loop

animate(0);
```

Interpolation and Smoothing

To achieve smooth and fluid animations, it's often necessary to interpolate between animation states. Linear interpolation (LERP) is a common technique for smoothly transitioning between positions, rotations, or other properties over time. LERP ensures that objects move evenly from one point to another, making animations look more natural.

Here's a simplified example of linear interpolation in WebGL:

```
// Example of linear interpolation (LERP)

function lerp(start, end, t) {

return (1 - t) * start + t * end;

}

// Interpolate position using LERP

function updatePosition(deltaTime) {

const t = Math.min(1, elapsedTime / animationDuration); // Ensure t doesn't exceed 1

const interpolatedX = lerp(startX, endX, t);

const interpolatedY = lerp(startY, endY, t);
```

```
// Update object's position
object.position.set(interpolatedX, interpolatedY, 0);
}
```

Frame Rate Optimization

To maintain a consistent frame rate in graphics applications, it's essential to optimize your code. This includes minimizing rendering and computation overhead. Techniques like frustum culling, level of detail (LOD), and occlusion culling can help improve performance, especially when dealing with complex scenes or large numbers of objects.

Additionally, consider using graphics libraries and hardware acceleration to offload rendering tasks to the GPU, which can significantly improve animation performance.

User Interaction and Feedback

Smooth animations can enhance the user experience, especially in interactive applications. Providing responsive feedback to user interactions, such as mouse movements or touch gestures, can make animations feel more intuitive and engaging.

In WebGL, you can use event listeners to capture user input and trigger animations or interactions based on user actions. For example, you might implement smooth camera panning in response to a swipe gesture on a touch screen.

Conclusion

Creating smooth animations in both OpenGL and WebGL environments involves careful timing, interpolation, and optimization. By ensuring a consistent frame rate, using delta time, and employing interpolation techniques, you can achieve animations that are visually pleasing and responsive to user input. Smooth animations enhance the overall quality and usability of your graphics applications, contributing to a more immersive user experience.

Chapter 9: Optimization Strategies

Section 9.1: Performance Considerations in Graphics Programming

When developing graphics applications using OpenGL or WebGL, performance optimization is a critical aspect of ensuring that your application runs smoothly and efficiently. In this section, we will explore various performance considerations and strategies that can help you achieve optimal performance in your graphics programs.

1. Render Batching

One of the key strategies for optimizing graphics performance is render batching. This involves grouping similar objects or geometry together and rendering them in a single draw call. In OpenGL and WebGL, reducing the number of draw calls can significantly improve performance. Use techniques like instanced rendering or vertex array objects (VAOs) to efficiently batch your rendering operations.

2. Level of Detail (LOD)

LOD techniques involve using lower-detail models or textures for objects that are farther away from the camera. This reduces the amount of data that needs to be processed and rendered, improving performance. LOD is especially useful in scenes with many objects or complex 3D models.

3. Shader Optimization

Shaders are at the heart of modern graphics programming. Optimizing your shaders can lead to substantial performance gains. Consider techniques such as minimizing shader complexity, avoiding unnecessary calculations, and using shader uniforms efficiently. Additionally, explore shader compilation and linking optimizations to reduce load times.

4. Texture Atlases

Efficient texture management is crucial in graphics programming. Texture atlases are a technique where multiple textures are packed into a single texture, reducing the number of texture binds and improving rendering efficiency. Use texture atlases for sprites, fonts, or any situation with multiple textures.

5. Geometry Instancing

When rendering multiple instances of the same object with the same geometry but different transformations (e.g., rendering multiple trees in a forest scene), consider using geometry instancing. This technique allows you to draw multiple instances with a single draw call, reducing CPU overhead.

6. Frustrum Culling and Occlusion Culling

Eliminating objects that are not visible to the camera can significantly improve rendering performance. Implement techniques like frustum culling to remove objects outside the camera's view frustum and occlusion culling to avoid rendering objects hidden by others.

7. GPU Acceleration

Utilize the power of the GPU for rendering tasks whenever possible. OpenGL and WebGL are designed to leverage GPU hardware for graphics operations. Make use of vertex and fragment shaders to offload computations to the GPU, which can lead to substantial performance improvements.

8. Resource Management

Efficient resource management is essential for good performance. Avoid unnecessary memory allocations and deallocate resources when they are no longer needed. Use resource pools and object pooling to recycle resources like textures or buffers.

9. Profile and Benchmark

Profiling your graphics application is crucial for identifying bottlenecks and performance issues. Use profiling tools and libraries to measure frame rates, GPU usage, and CPU usage. Benchmarking can help you track performance improvements or regressions over time.

10. Cross-Platform Optimization

If you are targeting multiple platforms, consider platform-specific optimizations. Different GPUs and hardware configurations may require specific tweaks to achieve optimal performance on each platform.

Optimizing graphics performance in OpenGL and WebGL is an ongoing process. It involves a combination of techniques, careful measurement, and iterative refinement. By considering these strategies and continuously monitoring your application's performance, you can create graphics applications that deliver a smooth and responsive user experience.

Section 9.2: Optimizing OpenGL Applications

Optimizing OpenGL applications is crucial for achieving smooth and efficient graphics rendering. In this section, we will delve into specific strategies and techniques for optimizing OpenGL-based graphics programs.

1. Use Vertex Buffer Objects (VBOs) and Vertex Array Objects (VAOs)

VBOs and VAOs allow you to efficiently store and manage vertex data on the GPU, reducing the overhead of transferring data between CPU and GPU memory. By using these OpenGL features, you can minimize the CPU workload and improve rendering performance.

```
// Create and bind a Vertex Array Object (VAO)

GLuint vao;

glGenVertexArrays(1, &vao);

glBindVertexArray(vao);

// Create and bind a Vertex Buffer Object (VBO)

GLuint vbo;

glGenBuffers(1, &vbo);

glBindBuffer(GL_ARRAY_BUFFER, vbo);

// Load vertex data into the VBO

glBufferData(GL_ARRAY_BUFFER, sizeof(vertices), vertices, GL_STATIC_DRAW);
```

```
// Specify vertex attribute pointers

glVertexAttribPointer(0, 3, GL_FLOAT, GL_FALSE, 6 * sizeof(float), (void*)0);

glEnableVertexAttribArray(0);

// Unbind VAO and VBO

glBindVertexArray(0);

glBindBuffer(GL_ARRAY_BUFFER, 0);
```

2. Minimize State Changes

OpenGL retains a significant amount of rendering state information. Minimizing state changes, such as shader, texture, and buffer bindings, can improve performance. Group similar rendering operations together to reduce the number of state changes between draw calls.

3. Use Display Lists (Legacy OpenGL)

In legacy OpenGL (pre-OpenGL 3.0), display lists can be used to compile and store sequences of OpenGL commands. Although display lists are not part of modern OpenGL, they can still be beneficial for optimizing older applications.

```
GLuint list = glGenLists(1);

glNewList(list, GL_COMPILE);

// OpenGL commands (e.g., glVertex, glDrawArrays)

glEndList();

// Call the display list
```

```
glCallList(list);

// Delete the display list when no longer needed

glDeleteLists(list, 1);
```

4. Texture Compression

Compressing textures can reduce memory usage and improve texture loading times. OpenGL supports various texture compression formats like DXT and ETC. Use tools to generate compressed textures and load them efficiently.

5. Level of Detail (LOD)

Implement LOD techniques to reduce the level of detail for objects that are farther from the camera. This can significantly reduce the number of vertices and fragments processed, improving frame rates.

6. Cull Backfaces

Enable backface culling (e.g., glEnable(GL_CULL_FACE)) when rendering opaque objects. This prevents the rendering of faces that are not visible and can save processing time.

7. Batch Rendering

Group similar objects together and render them in a single draw call. This reduces the overhead of making multiple draw calls and improves rendering efficiency.

8. Asynchronous Loading

Load textures, models, and shaders asynchronously to avoid blocking the main thread. Asynchronous loading can help maintain a smooth frame rate by minimizing stalls during resource loading.

9. Shader Optimization

Optimize your shaders for performance by minimizing redundant calculations and avoiding unnecessary branches. Profiling shader performance can help identify bottlenecks.

10. Memory Management

Efficient memory management is essential. Avoid memory leaks and unnecessary allocations. Use object pooling to recycle resources like shaders, textures, and buffers.

Optimizing OpenGL applications requires a combination of careful design, profiling, and iterative refinement. By following these optimization strategies, you can create graphics applications that deliver high performance and a smooth user experience. Keep in mind that specific optimizations may vary depending on your application's requirements and target platform.

Section 9.3: Optimizing WebGL for Performance

Optimizing WebGL applications is essential to ensure a smooth and responsive user experience in web-based graphics programming. In this section, we will explore various techniques and best practices for optimizing the performance of WebGL applications.

1. Use RequestAnimationFrame

When animating WebGL content, prefer using the requestAnimationFrame API over setInterval or setTimeout. requestAnimationFrame syncs with the browser's rendering loop, ensuring smooth and efficient animations while minimizing unnecessary rendering when the tab is inactive.

```
function animate() {
// Update and render your WebGL scene here
requestAnimationFrame(animate);
}
animate(); // Start the animation loop
```

2. Minimize WebGL Context Loss

WebGL context loss can occur, especially when the user switches tabs or minimizes the browser window. Handle context loss gracefully by recreating WebGL resources (textures, buffers, shaders) and restoring the application state when the context is restored.

3. Batch WebGL Draw Calls

Similar to OpenGL, WebGL benefits from reducing the number of draw calls. Grouping objects with the same shader and texture into a single draw call can significantly improve rendering performance.

4. Use Efficient Data Formats

Optimize data transfer between JavaScript and WebGL by using typed arrays, such as Float32Array for vertex data. Minimize data conversion and copying to achieve better performance.

5. Texture Atlases and Texture Compression

Just like OpenGL, WebGL applications can benefit from texture atlases to reduce the number of texture switches. Additionally, consider using texture compression formats like ETC1/2 or PVRTC to reduce memory usage and loading times.

6. Mipmap Levels

Generate and use mipmaps for textures to improve rendering quality and performance when textures are viewed from different distances.

7. Shader Compilation and Linking

Precompile shaders whenever possible and avoid compiling shaders during runtime. Link shaders with the same program for multiple objects to reduce overhead.

8. Avoid Synchronous Operations

WebGL operates asynchronously, and synchronous operations can introduce stalls in rendering. Avoid synchronous file loading, texture uploads, or other blocking operations.

9. Use Transform Feedback (if applicable)

Transform feedback allows you to capture the results of vertex shader processing, enabling advanced effects like GPU-based particle systems and physics simulations.

10. Profile and Debug

Utilize browser developer tools, WebGL debugging extensions, and third-party profiling tools to identify performance bottlenecks. Profiling can help you pinpoint areas that require optimization.

11. WebGL Extensions

WebGL extensions provide additional functionality and optimization opportunities. However, use them judiciously, as not all platforms and browsers support the same set of extensions.

12. Reduce Overdraw

Minimize overdraw by sorting and rendering opaque objects from front to back. This reduces the number of unnecessary pixel shader executions.

Optimizing WebGL for performance involves a combination of careful coding practices, resource management, and performance profiling. Regularly testing and profiling your WebGL application on various devices and browsers will help you identify and address performance bottlenecks. Keep in mind that the specific optimization techniques may vary depending on the complexity and requirements of your WebGL project.

Section 9.4: Cross-Platform Optimization Techniques

Cross-platform optimization is crucial when developing graphics applications that target a wide range of devices and operating systems. This section explores various techniques for optimizing WebGL and OpenGL applications to ensure consistent performance across different platforms.

1. Device Detection

Start by detecting the user's device and capabilities. JavaScript libraries like Modernizr[1] can help determine which features and extensions are supported by the user's device. Use this information to select appropriate rendering techniques and settings.

```
if (Modernizr.webgl) {
// WebGL is supported
```

1. https://modernizr.com/

```
if (Modernizr.webgl2) {
// Use WebGL 2.0 features
} else {
// Use WebGL 1.0 features
}
} else {
// WebGL is not supported, use a fallback or notify the user
}
```

2. Fallbacks and Progressive Enhancement

Implement fallback mechanisms for devices that do not support WebGL. This can include displaying a 2D version of your content or providing alternative functionality. Conversely, use progressive enhancement to improve the experience for devices with better capabilities.

3. Resolution and Quality Levels

Allow users to adjust rendering quality and resolution settings based on their device's capabilities. Provide options for lower-end devices to reduce the graphical load while offering higher quality for powerful hardware.

4. Adaptive Rendering

Implement adaptive rendering techniques that adjust rendering complexity based on the user's device. This might involve reducing the number of graphical effects, lowering texture resolutions, or simplifying geometry for less capable devices.

5. Responsive Design

Ensure that your graphics application adapts to different screen sizes and orientations. Implement responsive design principles to make the user interface and graphics elements look and perform well on both desktop and mobile devices.

6. Testing Across Platforms

Regularly test your application on various devices, browsers, and operating systems to identify platform-specific issues. Emulators and remote debugging tools can be valuable for testing on a wide range of configurations.

7. Platform-Specific Optimization

Optimize specific parts of your code for different platforms when necessary. Some platforms may have quirks or performance bottlenecks that require tailored solutions.

8. WebGL Extensions and Fallbacks

While WebGL extensions can enhance performance, be mindful of their availability on different platforms. Implement fallbacks or alternative methods for platforms that lack support for specific extensions.

9. Cross-Browser Compatibility

Ensure that your graphics application works consistently across popular web browsers. Browser-specific issues can arise, so testing on multiple browsers is essential.

10. User Feedback

Collect feedback from users on different platforms to identify performance issues and usability problems. This feedback can guide further optimization efforts.

11. Continuous Optimization

Optimization is an ongoing process. As new devices and browser versions emerge, revisit your application to ensure it maintains optimal performance on the latest platforms.

Optimizing for cross-platform compatibility requires a balance between providing a visually rich experience and ensuring performance on a variety of devices. By implementing these techniques and staying vigilant about platform-specific challenges, you can deliver a consistent and enjoyable graphics application across different platforms and environments.

Section 9.5: Debugging and Profiling Graphics Applications

Debugging and profiling are essential steps in the development of WebGL and OpenGL applications to ensure optimal performance and identify and fix issues. This section explores various techniques and tools for debugging and profiling graphics applications.

1. Browser Developer Tools

Most modern web browsers come with developer tools that include a variety of useful features for debugging and profiling WebGL and OpenGL applications. You can inspect the DOM, monitor network activity, and access the JavaScript console for error messages and debugging output.

```
// Example of using console.log() for debugging

console.log('Debugging message:', variableName);
```

2. WebGL Inspector

WebGL Inspector[2] is a browser extension that provides in-depth debugging capabilities for WebGL applications. It allows you to inspect and modify shaders, textures, buffers, and more in real-time.

3. OpenGL Debugging Tools

For OpenGL applications, various debugging tools are available, such as OpenGL Debugger (gDEBugger)[3] and RenderDoc[4]. These tools enable you to analyze OpenGL function calls, inspect textures and shaders, and capture frames for later analysis.

4. Profiling Tools

Profiling tools help identify performance bottlenecks in your graphics application. They provide insights into CPU and GPU utilization, frame rates, and rendering times. Tools like Chrome DevTools[5] and Firefox Performance Tools[6] offer profiling capabilities.

5. Shader Debugging

Debugging shaders can be challenging but is crucial for identifying rendering issues. WebGL shader debugging tools like Spector.js[7] and

2. https://benvanik.github.io/WebGL-Inspector/
3. https://developer.nvidia.com/gdebugger
4. https://renderdoc.org/
5. https://developers.google.com/web/tools/chrome-devtools
6. https://developer.mozilla.org/en-US/docs/Tools/Performance
7. https://spector.babylonjs.com/

ShaderToy[8] can help you inspect shader code, uniforms, and attributes.

6. Frame Capture and Analysis

Capture frames of your graphics application and analyze them to identify rendering problems. Tools like Apitrace[9] and RenderDoc[10] allow you to capture frames and step through the rendering process.

7. GPU Profiling

Use GPU profiling tools like NVIDIA Nsight[11] or AMD Radeon GPU Profiler[12] to monitor GPU performance and identify bottlenecks specific to the graphics hardware.

8. Error Handling

Implement robust error handling in your WebGL and OpenGL code. Check for errors after each OpenGL or WebGL function call and log meaningful error messages.

```
// WebGL error handling

const gl = canvas.getContext('webgl');

if (!gl) {

console.error('WebGL is not supported on this device.');

}
```

8. https://www.shadertoy.com/

9. https://apitrace.github.io/

10. https://renderdoc.org/

11. https://developer.nvidia.com/nsight-graphics

12. https://gpuopen.com/gaming-product/rdna-gpu-architecture/

9. Logging and Tracing

Use logging and tracing mechanisms to track the flow of your graphics application. Log important events and timestamps to help diagnose issues and performance bottlenecks.

```
// Example of timestamping for tracing
console.time('FunctionName');
// Code to profile
console.timeEnd('FunctionName');
```

10. User Testing

Enlist users to test your graphics application on various devices and report any issues they encounter. Real-world testing can uncover issues that may not be apparent during development.

11. Continuous Testing

Integrate continuous testing into your development pipeline to catch regressions early. Automated testing scripts can run your graphics application on different configurations and report any failures.

Effective debugging and profiling practices are crucial for delivering high-quality graphics applications. By utilizing the right tools and techniques, you can identify and resolve issues, optimize performance, and provide a smooth and reliable user experience.

Chapter 10: Bridging Technologies

Section 10.1: The Need for Integration Between OpenGL and WebGL

The field of graphics programming is diverse, and developers often need to work with different technologies to achieve their goals. Two prominent technologies for graphics development are OpenGL and WebGL. While both serve similar purposes, they target different platforms and have distinct characteristics. This section explores the need for integration between OpenGL and WebGL, highlighting the scenarios where such integration can be beneficial.

1. Platform Diversity

OpenGL primarily targets desktop and native applications, whereas WebGL is designed for web browsers. Developers often need to create applications that run seamlessly on both platforms to reach a broader audience. Bridging technologies can help facilitate this cross-platform compatibility.

2. Code Reusability

Leveraging existing OpenGL codebases and adapting them for use in WebGL can save significant development time and effort. Bridging technologies enable the reuse of OpenGL code, allowing developers to bring their desktop applications to the web without starting from scratch.

3. Performance Considerations

While WebGL is powerful, it operates within the constraints of web browsers and JavaScript engines. Certain performance optimizations and rendering techniques available in OpenGL may not have direct equivalents in WebGL. Bridging technologies can bridge this performance gap by translating OpenGL-specific optimizations into WebGL-compatible code.

4. Transitioning from Legacy Applications

Many legacy desktop applications are built using OpenGL. To modernize and extend the reach of these applications to the web, developers can utilize bridging technologies to facilitate the transition to WebGL gradually.

5. Cross-Platform Development

Developing for multiple platforms often involves writing separate codebases for each platform, leading to increased maintenance overhead. Bridging technologies enable cross-platform development, allowing developers to maintain a single codebase for both desktop and web applications.

6. Access to Web Features

WebGL applications can benefit from web-specific features such as HTML, CSS, and JavaScript integration. Bridging technologies enable OpenGL applications to harness these web features while preserving their core graphics functionality.

7. Rich User Experiences

Integrating WebGL into existing OpenGL applications can enhance user experiences by enabling interactive web-based features, such as 3D product configurators, online gaming, and collaborative 3D modeling.

8. Compatibility Challenges

While OpenGL and WebGL share similarities, they also have differences in their APIs and capabilities. Bridging technologies must address these differences to ensure a smooth transition between the two, which can be a challenging task.

In summary, the need for integration between OpenGL and WebGL arises from the desire to create cross-platform graphics applications that leverage the strengths of both technologies. Bridging technologies play a crucial role in achieving this integration, allowing developers to reuse code, optimize performance, and deliver rich user experiences on both desktop and web platforms. This chapter explores tools, libraries, and techniques that facilitate the bridging of OpenGL and WebGL, along with real-world case studies showcasing successful integrations.

Section 10.2: Tools and Libraries for Bridging the Gap

To bridge the gap between OpenGL and WebGL effectively, developers can leverage various tools and libraries that simplify the process and provide compatibility across different platforms. These tools and libraries offer a range of features, from automated code translation to cross-platform rendering support. In this section, we'll explore some of the most popular tools and libraries used for integrating OpenGL with WebGL.

1. Emscripten

Emscripten[1] is a widely used tool for compiling C and C++ code, including OpenGL applications, into WebAssembly (Wasm) and JavaScript. It provides a straightforward way to port existing

1. https://emscripten.org/

OpenGL applications to the web. Emscripten's capabilities include OpenGL to WebGL translation, allowing developers to maintain a single codebase for both desktop and web platforms.

2. WebGLU

WebGLU[2] is a library specifically designed for bridging OpenGL and WebGL. It offers a set of utilities and abstractions that simplify the process of adapting OpenGL code for the web. WebGLU provides functions for translating OpenGL shaders and handling WebGL-specific tasks, making it easier to port existing code.

3. Regal

Regal[3] is an OpenGL abstraction layer that can help bridge the gap between OpenGL and WebGL. It provides OpenGL compatibility and a set of extensions, allowing developers to use OpenGL features not directly available in WebGL. Regal can be particularly useful for applications that rely on advanced OpenGL functionalities.

4. GLOVE

GLOVE[4] is a lightweight library that aims to simplify OpenGL to WebGL translation. It provides an API that closely resembles OpenGL, allowing developers to write code in a familiar way while targeting the web. GLOVE focuses on ease of use and aims to minimize the effort required for porting OpenGL applications to WebGL.

---

2. https://github.com/WebGLTools/WebGLU
3. https://github.com/p3/regal
4. https://github.com/roarmstrong/glove

5. three.js

three.js[5] is a popular 3D graphics library for JavaScript that abstracts the complexities of WebGL. While not a direct bridge between OpenGL and WebGL, it offers a high-level API that simplifies 3D graphics programming in the web environment. Developers can use three.js to create interactive 3D applications that run smoothly in web browsers.

6. Babylon.js

Babylon.js[6] is another JavaScript-based 3D engine that provides an alternative to WebGL for web-based graphics. It includes a wide range of features for creating 3D scenes, animations, and games. Developers can use Babylon.js to build immersive experiences on the web while abstracting the underlying WebGL code.

7. WebGL Wrappers

Several wrapper libraries and frameworks, such as pywebgl[7], PyOpenGL[8], and OGL[9], aim to simplify WebGL development by providing high-level abstractions and utilities. While these wrappers may not directly bridge OpenGL code, they offer a convenient way to work with WebGL and create web-based graphics applications.

8. Custom Solutions

In some cases, developers may opt for custom solutions tailored to their specific needs. This approach involves manually adapting

---

5. https://threejs.org/

6. https://www.babylonjs.com/

7. https://github.com/stackgl/pywebgl

8. http://pyopengl.sourceforge.net/

9. https://github.com/oframe/ogl

OpenGL code to WebGL by writing translation layers and shaders. While it requires more effort, it provides full control over the integration process and allows for fine-tuning performance optimizations.

Choosing the right tool or library for bridging OpenGL and WebGL depends on the complexity of the project, the level of control needed, and the existing codebase. Developers should evaluate these options and consider factors such as ease of use, performance, and community support when making their selection. Successful integration between OpenGL and WebGL can open up new possibilities for cross-platform graphics applications, making it a valuable endeavor for developers in the field of graphics programming.

Section 10.3: Case Studies: Successful OpenGL-WebGL Integrations

In this section, we'll delve into real-world case studies of successful integrations between OpenGL and WebGL. These examples demonstrate the practical applications and benefits of bridging these two graphics technologies.

1. Unity3D

Unity3D[10] is a widely used game development platform that originally targeted desktop and console platforms using OpenGL. However, with the advent of WebGL, Unity Technologies introduced WebGL export support, allowing developers to deploy Unity games directly in web browsers. This integration is seamless, and Unity handles the translation of OpenGL rendering calls to

10. https://unity.com/

WebGL, making it easier for game developers to reach a broader audience.

2. Blender

Blender[11], a popular open-source 3D modeling and animation software, has incorporated WebGL support into its platform. Users can now export 3D models and animations directly to WebGL, enabling interactive 3D content creation for the web. This integration opens up new possibilities for artists and designers to showcase their work in an accessible online format.

3. Mozilla Firefox

Web browsers like Mozilla Firefox[12] have integrated WebGL to provide hardware-accelerated 3D graphics directly within the browser environment. While not an OpenGL-to-WebGL bridge in the traditional sense, this integration showcases how major software projects can adopt WebGL to enhance the web browsing experience. WebGL allows websites to render complex 3D content without requiring users to install additional plugins.

4. Unreal Engine

Unreal Engine[13] is a powerful game engine that initially targeted OpenGL for desktop platforms. With the growth of WebGL, Epic Games introduced WebGL export capabilities. Game developers can now create and export Unreal Engine games for web browsers, reaching a broader audience without significant code changes.

---

11. https://www.blender.org/

12. https://www.mozilla.org/en-US/firefox/new/

13. https://www.unrealengine.com/

5. Gloo

Gloo[14] is an open-source C++ library that simplifies the process of bridging OpenGL and WebGL. It has been used in various projects, including LibIGL[15], a popular C++ library for geometry processing. By integrating Gloo, these projects enable users to visualize and interact with 3D models in web browsers, promoting accessibility and collaboration.

6. Interactive Data Visualization

Numerous data visualization tools and libraries leverage WebGL to create interactive and performant charts, graphs, and simulations. Libraries like D3.js[16] and Three.js[17] enable developers to build web-based data visualization applications that take advantage of GPU acceleration, offering a smooth user experience for exploring complex datasets.

7. Educational Content

Educational platforms and institutions have adopted WebGL to deliver interactive 3D content to students and learners worldwide. Whether for teaching physics concepts through simulations or exploring historical sites in 3D, WebGL integration has revolutionized the way educational content is presented and consumed online.

These case studies highlight the versatility and impact of bridging OpenGL and WebGL. Whether in the gaming industry, content creation, web browsing, or education, the integration of these

---

14. https://github.com/alecjacobson/gloo

15. https://libigl.github.io/libigl/

16. https://d3js.org/

17. https://threejs.org/

technologies enables developers and creators to bring high-quality 3D graphics to a broader audience on the web. As WebGL continues to evolve and gain wider support, we can expect even more innovative applications that leverage the strengths of both OpenGL and WebGL.

Section 10.4: Challenges in Bridging Technologies

While integrating OpenGL and WebGL offers numerous benefits, it also comes with its set of challenges and considerations. In this section, we'll explore some of the common challenges developers may encounter when bridging these two graphics technologies.

1. Platform Compatibility

One of the primary challenges is ensuring cross-platform compatibility. OpenGL traditionally targets desktop and native environments, whereas WebGL runs in web browsers across various operating systems and devices. Developers must account for differences in graphics drivers, browser implementations, and hardware capabilities, which can lead to compatibility issues.

2. Performance Optimization

Performance optimization can be complex when transitioning from OpenGL to WebGL. WebGL operates in a sandboxed environment with limitations imposed by the web browser, which can affect performance compared to native OpenGL applications. Developers need to fine-tune their code to maximize performance while maintaining visual fidelity.

3. Security Concerns

WebGL's integration into web browsers introduces security considerations. WebGL exposes the GPU to web content, potentially allowing malicious websites to exploit vulnerabilities. Browser vendors implement security measures to mitigate risks, but developers should also adopt best practices for secure WebGL applications.

4. Shader Translation

Translating OpenGL shaders to WebGL shaders can be challenging due to differences in the shading languages and APIs. WebGL uses GLSL ES, a subset of OpenGL's GLSL. Developers may need to adapt or rewrite shaders to ensure they function correctly in a web context.

5. Resource Management

Managing resources such as textures, buffers, and shaders can differ between OpenGL and WebGL. Developers need to be mindful of WebGL's resource limits and the need to handle resource creation, usage, and disposal efficiently.

6. Debugging and Profiling

Debugging and profiling WebGL applications can be more challenging than debugging native OpenGL applications. Tools and techniques used for debugging web content may differ from those for desktop development. Developers must be proficient in debugging WebGL-specific issues.

7. Learning Curve

Developers familiar with OpenGL may face a learning curve when transitioning to WebGL. While there are similarities, the web environment introduces unique concepts and limitations. Bridging the gap requires gaining expertise in both technologies.

8. Browser Support

WebGL's availability varies across web browsers, and the level of support for WebGL features may differ. Developers must consider browser compatibility and provide fallbacks or alternatives when necessary to ensure a consistent user experience.

9. Updates and Evolving Standards

Both OpenGL and WebGL continue to evolve, with new features and extensions being introduced. Developers need to stay up-to-date with changes in the standards and adjust their code accordingly.

10. Community and Documentation

Finding resources, documentation, and community support for OpenGL and WebGL can be challenging, especially for bridging technologies. Developers may need to rely on a combination of OpenGL and WebGL resources to address specific integration issues.

Despite these challenges, the benefits of bridging OpenGL and WebGL are substantial, enabling developers to reach a broader audience with interactive 3D graphics on the web. By understanding and addressing these challenges, developers can create successful integrations that offer engaging and performant web experiences.

Section 10.5: Future of Integrated Graphics Programming

The integration of OpenGL and WebGL represents a significant milestone in the world of graphics programming, and it opens up exciting possibilities for the future. In this section, we'll explore some potential directions and trends for integrated graphics programming.

1. Unified Graphics APIs

One possible future trend is the development of unified graphics APIs that bridge the gap between desktop and web environments. This could lead to more seamless transitions between OpenGL and WebGL, reducing the complexities of integration and ensuring consistent performance and capabilities across platforms.

2. Improved WebGL Performance

As web browsers continue to evolve, we can expect improvements in WebGL performance. Browser vendors are actively working to optimize the execution of WebGL code, making it more competitive with native OpenGL performance. This will further blur the line between web and desktop graphics applications.

3. WebGPU Integration

WebGPU is an emerging web standard designed to provide lower-level access to GPU hardware, similar to OpenGL and Vulkan. The integration of WebGPU into web browsers could simplify the development of high-performance graphics applications that run seamlessly on the web.

4. Enhanced Tooling and Debugging

Developers can anticipate better tooling and debugging support for integrated graphics programming. This includes integrated development environments (IDEs) that seamlessly handle both OpenGL and WebGL code, as well as advanced debugging tools tailored for web-based graphics.

5. Advanced Cross-Compilation Tools

Cross-compilation tools that convert OpenGL code to WebGL, and vice versa, may become more sophisticated. These tools will help bridge the gap further and reduce the manual effort required for porting graphics applications between platforms.

6. Augmented and Virtual Reality on the Web

The combination of WebGL and emerging web technologies could pave the way for immersive augmented reality (AR) and virtual reality (VR) experiences directly in web browsers. This would bring graphics programming to the forefront of web-based interactive content.

7. Machine Learning Integration

Graphics programming is increasingly intersecting with machine learning and artificial intelligence. Future developments may involve integrating machine learning models and techniques directly into graphics pipelines for more realistic and interactive graphics.

8. Accessibility and Inclusivity

The future of integrated graphics programming should prioritize accessibility and inclusivity. Developers will need to consider various user devices, input methods, and assistive technologies to ensure that their graphics applications are usable by all.

9. Standardization Efforts

Standardization efforts will continue to shape the landscape of integrated graphics programming. Industry standards bodies and organizations will play a crucial role in defining best practices and ensuring compatibility between different graphics technologies.

10. Collaboration and Community Growth

The graphics programming community will continue to grow and collaborate on open source projects, sharing knowledge and resources to address the challenges of integrated graphics development. This sense of community is essential for driving innovation in the field.

In conclusion, the future of integrated graphics programming holds immense promise, enabling developers to create captivating and high-performance graphics applications that span both desktop and web environments. As technology continues to advance, it's an exciting time for those interested in pushing the boundaries of interactive graphics on the web.

Chapter 11: WebGL in Modern Web Development

Section 11.1: Role of WebGL in Contemporary Web Design

WebGL has become an integral part of modern web development, revolutionizing the way we interact with websites and applications. Its role in contemporary web design is profound, offering a new dimension of interactivity and realism to web experiences. In this section, we will delve into the significance of WebGL in shaping the modern web landscape.

Enhancing User Engagement

One of the primary roles of WebGL in contemporary web design is enhancing user engagement. With WebGL, developers can create immersive 3D environments and interactive simulations that captivate users. Whether it's a product configurator, a virtual tour, or a game-like experience, WebGL enables websites to hold users' attention and make their visit memorable.

Data Visualization

WebGL is a powerful tool for data visualization, allowing complex datasets to be presented in a visually appealing and comprehensible manner. Through WebGL-powered charts, graphs, and interactive visualizations, users can explore and gain insights from data right within their web browsers. This capability is crucial for industries such as finance, healthcare, and science.

Gaming and Entertainment

The gaming and entertainment industry has greatly benefited from WebGL. Browser-based games with console-quality graphics and performance are now a reality. WebGL enables developers to create stunning 3D games that users can enjoy without the need for plugins or downloads. This has democratized gaming and made it accessible to a broader audience.

Interactive Product Presentations

E-commerce websites leverage WebGL to provide interactive product presentations. Users can rotate, zoom, and explore products from all angles, closely simulating the physical shopping experience. This immersive approach helps users make informed purchase decisions and reduces the likelihood of returns.

Architectural and Interior Design

WebGL is invaluable in architectural and interior design. It allows architects and designers to showcase their projects in 3D, enabling clients to take virtual tours of buildings, homes, or interior spaces. This enhances communication, as clients can better visualize the end result and provide feedback.

Educational Simulations

Educational institutions and e-learning platforms use WebGL to create interactive simulations and virtual laboratories. These simulations enable students to conduct experiments, explore scientific concepts, and gain practical knowledge in a virtual environment, enhancing the quality of education.

Cross-Platform Compatibility

WebGL's role in contemporary web design is further accentuated by its cross-platform compatibility. It works seamlessly across various devices, including desktops, laptops, smartphones, and tablets. This ensures that the WebGL experiences designed by developers reach a wide audience, regardless of the device they use.

In summary, WebGL plays a pivotal role in contemporary web design by enhancing user engagement, enabling data visualization, powering gaming and entertainment experiences, facilitating interactive product presentations, aiding architectural and interior design, supporting educational simulations, and ensuring cross-platform compatibility. Its versatility and ability to deliver rich 3D content directly in web browsers make it an indispensable technology in the modern web development toolkit. In the following sections, we will explore how to integrate WebGL with HTML, CSS, JavaScript, and web frameworks to create captivating web experiences.

Section 11.2: Integrating WebGL with HTML and CSS

Integrating WebGL with HTML and CSS is a fundamental aspect of creating engaging web experiences. WebGL alone provides the power to render 3D graphics within a web browser, but it needs HTML and CSS to structure the content and style the interface. In this section, we'll explore how to seamlessly integrate WebGL into your web projects.

HTML Structure

To begin, let's look at how HTML can be used to structure a webpage with WebGL content. Typically, you would define a container element within your HTML where the WebGL content will be displayed. This container can be a <div>, a <canvas>, or any other HTML element that suits your design. For example:

```
<!DOCTYPE html>

<html>

<head>

<title>WebGL Integration</title>

</head>

<body>

<div id="webgl-container"></div>

</body>

</html>
```

In this example, we've created a <div> element with the id "webgl-container" to serve as the WebGL rendering area. This container can be styled using CSS to control its dimensions, position, and appearance.

CSS Styling

CSS is essential for styling both the WebGL container and the surrounding interface elements. You can use CSS to set the size, position, and background of the WebGL container, ensuring it fits seamlessly into your webpage's layout. For instance:

```
#webgl-container {

width: 100%;
```

```
height: 400px;

background-color: #000;

}
```

In this CSS snippet, we've set the width to 100% to make the container span the entire width of its parent element, and we've given it a height of 400 pixels. We've also specified a background color of black (#000), which is often used as a background for WebGL content. You can further customize the styles to match your project's aesthetics.

JavaScript Integration

Once you have the HTML structure and CSS styling in place, JavaScript is used to create and manipulate the WebGL context within the designated container. You can include your WebGL code directly in your HTML file or link to external JavaScript files where you've organized your WebGL logic.

Here's a simplified example of setting up a WebGL context within the "webgl-container" using JavaScript:

```
const canvas = document.createElement('canvas');

canvas.width = window.innerWidth;

canvas.height = 400;

document.getElementById('webgl-container').appendChild(canvas);

const gl = canvas.getContext('webgl');

if (!gl) {
```

```
console.error('WebGL not supported, falling back on experimental-webgl');

gl = canvas.getContext('experimental-webgl');

}

if (!gl) {

alert('Your browser does not support WebGL');

}

// Your WebGL rendering code goes here
```

In this JavaScript snippet, we first create a <canvas> element, set its dimensions to match the container, and append it to the "webgl-container." Then, we obtain the WebGL context using getContext() and perform error handling to ensure WebGL is supported in the user's browser.

After setting up the context, you can proceed to write your WebGL rendering code as needed for your project.

Interaction with HTML Elements

To create interactive WebGL experiences, you can integrate user interface elements, such as buttons, sliders, or forms, into your HTML structure. JavaScript can be used to handle user interactions and update the WebGL content accordingly. Libraries like Three.js and Babylon.js provide utilities to simplify this process.

In summary, integrating WebGL with HTML and CSS involves structuring your HTML to include a container for WebGL content, styling it with CSS, and using JavaScript to create and manipulate the WebGL context within that container. This integration allows you to seamlessly embed interactive 3D graphics into your web projects, providing engaging and immersive user experiences. In the next section, we will explore how to interact with WebGL using JavaScript and various web frameworks.

Section 11.3: Interaction with JavaScript and Web Frameworks

Interacting with WebGL using JavaScript and web frameworks is crucial for creating dynamic and responsive 3D web applications. This section explores how JavaScript and popular web frameworks can be used to enhance the interactivity and functionality of WebGL content.

JavaScript and WebGL Interaction

JavaScript plays a central role in controlling and updating WebGL scenes. It allows you to respond to user input, perform animations, and manipulate 3D objects in real-time. Here are some common tasks you can achieve through JavaScript:

1. **User Input Handling:** JavaScript can capture user interactions, such as mouse clicks, keyboard input, or touch events. You can use event listeners to respond to these interactions and trigger specific actions in your WebGL application.
2. **Animation:** By using JavaScript's requestAnimationFrame() function, you can create smooth animations in your WebGL scenes. This function ensures that animations are synchronized with the browser's rendering loop, providing a consistent and responsive user experience.
3. **Updating Scene Data:** JavaScript can dynamically update

the properties and positions of 3D objects in your WebGL scene. This is essential for interactive applications where objects need to move, rotate, or change appearance in response to user actions.

4. **Communication:** JavaScript enables communication between your WebGL application and external data sources or APIs. You can fetch data from a server, update textures, or synchronize your application with other web services.

Here's a simplified example of JavaScript code that responds to a button click event to change the color of a 3D object in a WebGL scene:

```
// Assuming you have a WebGL context 'gl' and a 3D object 'cube' defined

const colorButton = document.getElementById('change-color-button');

colorButton.addEventListener('click', () => {

const newColor = [Math.random(), Math.random(), Math.random(), 1.0]; // Generate a random color

gl.bindBuffer(gl.ARRAY_BUFFER, cube.colorBuffer);

gl.bufferData(gl.ARRAY_BUFFER, new Float32Array(newColor), gl.STATIC_DRAW);

});
```

In this example, when the "change-color-button" is clicked, JavaScript generates a random color and updates the color buffer of a 3D object, causing it to change color in the WebGL scene.

Web Frameworks and Libraries

Web frameworks and libraries can significantly simplify the development of WebGL applications. They provide pre-built components, abstractions, and tools that streamline common tasks. Some popular frameworks and libraries for WebGL development include:

1. **Three.js:** Three.js is a widely used 3D graphics library for JavaScript that abstracts many of the complexities of WebGL. It offers a high-level API for creating 3D scenes, handling camera controls, and loading 3D models. It's a great choice for both beginners and experienced developers.
2. **Babylon.js:** Babylon.js is another powerful JavaScript framework for building 3D applications. It provides a physics engine, particle system, and a wide range of features for creating interactive 3D experiences. It's suitable for gaming and simulations.
3. **A-Frame:** A-Frame is an open-source web framework that simplifies creating virtual reality (VR) and augmented reality (AR) experiences using HTML. It's built on top of Three.js and allows you to create VR and AR content with minimal code.
4. **regl:** If you prefer a more lightweight and minimalistic approach, regl is a low-level WebGL library that focuses on performance and efficiency. It's suitable for developers who want fine-grained control over their WebGL applications.

These frameworks and libraries provide a higher level of abstraction and often come with extensive documentation and communities, making it easier to get started with WebGL development and build complex 3D web applications.

Conclusion

JavaScript and web frameworks play a pivotal role in enhancing the interactivity and functionality of WebGL content. They enable you to create responsive and dynamic 3D web applications by handling user input, performing animations, updating scenes, and facilitating communication with external data sources. Whether you choose to work with raw WebGL or leverage the capabilities of popular frameworks, mastering JavaScript is essential for successful WebGL development. In the next section, we will explore responsive design and cross-browser compatibility when using WebGL in modern web development.

Section 11.4: Responsive Design and Cross-Browser Compatibility

Creating WebGL content that is responsive and compatible across various web browsers and devices is essential for ensuring a broad audience can access and enjoy your 3D web applications. This section delves into the principles of responsive design and strategies for achieving cross-browser compatibility.

Principles of Responsive Design

Responsive design is an approach that ensures web content adapts and scales gracefully to fit different screen sizes and orientations, from desktop monitors to smartphones and tablets. Here are key principles to consider when implementing responsive design for WebGL applications:

1. **Fluid Layouts:** Use flexible layout techniques like percentage-based widths and relative positioning to allow content to expand or contract based on the available screen

space.

2. **Media Queries:** Employ CSS media queries to apply different styles and configurations based on the user's device characteristics, such as screen width, resolution, and orientation. This enables you to tailor the presentation of your WebGL content to different devices.
3. **Viewport Settings:** Configure the viewport meta tag in your HTML to control how the browser renders the content on mobile devices. Setting the viewport width to the device width helps ensure proper scaling.
4. **Retina and High-DPI Displays:** Consider providing higher-resolution textures and assets for devices with high-density displays (e.g., Retina displays on Apple devices) to maintain image clarity.
5. **Touch and Mouse Interactions:** Adapt user interactions to support both touch and mouse input. Ensure that your WebGL application responds to gestures and clicks, as some users may be on touch-enabled devices while others use traditional input methods.

Cross-Browser Compatibility

Achieving cross-browser compatibility is crucial for ensuring that your WebGL content works consistently across different web browsers, such as Chrome, Firefox, Safari, Edge, and others. Here are strategies for addressing browser compatibility issues:

1. **Feature Detection:** Rather than browser detection, use feature detection to check if specific WebGL features and APIs are supported. Libraries like Modernizr can help with feature detection and graceful degradation.
2. **WebGL Polyfills:** Consider using WebGL polyfills or shims that provide WebGL-like functionality for browsers

that don't support WebGL natively. These can help extend compatibility to older browsers.

3. **Vendor Prefixes:** Some WebGL APIs may require vendor-specific prefixes for certain browsers. Be sure to include prefixes for WebGL functions to ensure compatibility with different browsers.
4. **Error Handling:** Implement robust error handling in your WebGL code to gracefully handle situations where WebGL is not supported or encounters issues. Provide meaningful error messages to users.
5. **Testing and Debugging:** Regularly test your WebGL application in multiple browsers and devices to identify and address compatibility issues. Browser developer tools and debugging libraries can aid in diagnosing problems.
6. **User Notifications:** Inform users when their browser or device may not fully support your WebGL content. Offer alternatives or guidance on how to enable WebGL if it's disabled.

Example of Media Query for Responsive Design

Here's an example of a CSS media query that adjusts the layout of a WebGL application based on the screen width:

```
/* Default styles for larger screens */

.canvas-container {

width: 100%;

}

/* Media query for screens with a maximum width of 768px (e.g., tablets and mobile devices) */
```

```
@media (max-width: 768px) {

.canvas-container {

width: 90%;

margin: 0 auto;

}

}
```

In this example, the .canvas-container element's width is adjusted to occupy 90% of the screen width when the screen width is 768 pixels or less. This ensures that the WebGL content remains readable and usable on smaller screens.

Conclusion

Responsive design and cross-browser compatibility are vital considerations when developing WebGL applications. By following these principles and strategies, you can ensure that your 3D web content is accessible and functional across a wide range of devices and browsers. In the next section, we will explore case studies of innovative WebGL websites to gain inspiration and insights into real-world WebGL applications.

Section 11.5: Case Studies: Innovative WebGL Websites

In this section, we'll explore several case studies of innovative WebGL websites that demonstrate the power and versatility of WebGL in modern web development. These examples showcase the creative possibilities of WebGL and provide inspiration for developers looking to leverage this technology for their projects.

1. Awwwards[1]

Awwwards[2] is a website that recognizes and celebrates the best in web design and development. It uses WebGL to create stunning 3D animations and interactive elements throughout its site. Visitors can explore a visually captivating and immersive experience as they navigate through the website's various sections.

2. The Rookies[3]

The Rookies[4] is a platform for aspiring digital artists, designers, and animators to showcase their portfolios and connect with industry professionals. WebGL is utilized to present 3D art and design projects in an interactive and engaging manner. Users can view and interact with 3D models and animations directly within their web browsers.

3. HelloRacer[5]

HelloRacer[6] is an online racing game that demonstrates WebGL's capabilities for gaming in the browser. It offers a high-quality, 3D racing experience directly within the web browser, showcasing smooth graphics, realistic physics, and multiplayer functionality. This example highlights WebGL's potential for creating browser-based games with console-level graphics.

---

1. https://www.awwwards.com/

2. https://www.awwwards.com/

3. https://www.therookies.co/

4. https://www.therookies.co/

5. https://helloracer.com/

6. https://helloracer.com/

4. Asos[7]

Asos[8] is a popular online fashion retailer that uses WebGL to enhance the shopping experience. WebGL is employed to create interactive 3D models of clothing items, allowing customers to rotate and inspect products from all angles. This feature helps shoppers make more informed purchasing decisions.

5. Space Spot[9]

Space Spot[10] is a website that allows users to track the International Space Station (ISS) in real-time. It leverages WebGL to display a 3D model of the ISS orbiting Earth, providing users with a visually appealing and educational experience. Users can see the current position of the ISS and track its path across the sky.

6. PlayCanvas[11]

PlayCanvas[12] is an online platform for creating and publishing 3D games and interactive experiences. The entire platform is built on WebGL technology, enabling users to develop games and simulations that can be run directly in web browsers. PlayCanvas demonstrates how WebGL can empower developers to build and share complex 3D applications online.

---

7. https://www.asos.com/

8. https://www.asos.com/

9. https://www.spotthespacestation.com/

10. https://www.spotthespacestation.com/

11. https://playcanvas.com/

12. https://playcanvas.com/

7. WebGL Fundamentals[13]

WebGL Fundamentals[14] is an educational website that teaches WebGL programming from the ground up. It provides interactive examples and tutorials for learning WebGL concepts and techniques. This website is an excellent resource for developers interested in diving into WebGL development.

These case studies illustrate the versatility and impact of WebGL in various domains, from web design and e-commerce to gaming and education. WebGL's ability to bring 3D graphics and interactive experiences to the web opens up exciting possibilities for creating engaging and immersive web content.

In conclusion, WebGL has become a fundamental technology for modern web development, enabling developers to push the boundaries of what's possible in web-based graphics and interactivity. As you embark on your own WebGL projects, draw inspiration from these innovative examples and explore the full potential of WebGL to create remarkable web experiences.

---

13. https://webglfundamentals.org/

14. https://webglfundamentals.org/

Chapter 12: Advanced Rendering Techniques

Section 12.1: Real-Time Rendering Concepts

In this section, we will delve into the fascinating world of real-time rendering and explore the fundamental concepts that underlie it. Real-time rendering is the process of generating and displaying images in a computer program or application at interactive rates, typically 30 frames per second (FPS) or higher. It plays a crucial role in modern graphics applications, including video games, simulations, and virtual reality. Understanding the principles of real-time rendering is essential for achieving visually stunning and responsive graphics.

Key Concepts in Real-Time Rendering:

1. **Frame Rate (FPS):** Frame rate is the number of frames or images displayed per second. In real-time rendering, achieving a consistent and high frame rate is critical to providing smooth and responsive visuals. Frame rate can be affected by the complexity of the scene, rendering techniques, and hardware capabilities.
2. **Rasterization:** Rasterization is the process of converting 3D geometry and objects into 2D pixels on the screen. It involves determining which objects and parts of objects are visible and then mapping them to the screen. Rasterization is a fundamental step in rendering pipelines.
3. **Shading:** Shading is the process of determining the color and brightness of pixels on the screen. It involves simulating the interaction of light with surfaces, materials, and objects in the scene. Shaders, which we explored in

previous chapters, are a vital tool for achieving realistic shading effects.

4. **Texture Mapping:** Texture mapping is the process of applying 2D images (textures) to 3D objects to enhance their appearance. Textures can contain color information, patterns, and details that make surfaces appear more realistic. Proper texture mapping is crucial for achieving high-quality visuals.
5. **Lighting Models:** Lighting models simulate how light interacts with surfaces to determine their appearance. Real-time rendering often employs simplified lighting models to calculate the reflection of light on objects. These models can include ambient, diffuse, specular, and other components.
6. **Anti-Aliasing:** Anti-aliasing techniques are used to reduce the jagged or "staircase" appearance of diagonal or curved lines in rendered images. These techniques smooth out edges and improve image quality.
7. **Shadow Mapping:** Shadows are essential for creating depth and realism in scenes. Shadow mapping is a technique used to simulate the casting and rendering of shadows in real-time graphics.
8. **Post-Processing Effects:** Post-processing effects, such as bloom, motion blur, and depth of field, are applied to rendered frames after the initial rendering process. These effects can significantly enhance the visual appeal of a scene.
9. **Level of Detail (LOD):** LOD techniques involve dynamically adjusting the detail of objects in the scene based on their distance from the viewer. This optimization helps maintain a high frame rate by reducing the computational load when objects are distant and less

visible.

10. **Rendering APIs:** Real-time rendering relies on graphics APIs like OpenGL and WebGL, which provide a set of functions and tools for interacting with the GPU and rendering hardware. These APIs enable developers to harness the power of modern graphics hardware for real-time rendering.

In the world of real-time rendering, achieving a balance between visual quality and performance is a constant challenge. Developers must optimize their rendering pipelines, utilize efficient algorithms, and make creative use of shaders to create captivating visuals while ensuring a smooth user experience. As we explore advanced rendering techniques in the upcoming sections of this chapter, we will delve deeper into these concepts and learn how to apply them effectively in OpenGL and WebGL applications.

Section 12.2: Advanced OpenGL Rendering Techniques

In this section, we'll explore advanced OpenGL rendering techniques that go beyond the basics covered in earlier chapters. These techniques are crucial for achieving sophisticated and visually impressive graphics in your applications. We'll discuss various topics, including framebuffers, multi-pass rendering, and post-processing effects.

Framebuffers and Renderbuffers

Framebuffers are essential components in OpenGL for off-screen rendering. They allow you to render a scene to a texture or image rather than directly to the screen. This capability is fundamental for implementing post-processing effects, shadow mapping, and other advanced techniques.

A framebuffer is composed of multiple attachments, which can be textures or renderbuffers. These attachments store different types of data, such as color information, depth values, and stencil information. By rendering to specific attachments, you can perform various rendering passes and combine the results to achieve complex visual effects.

Here's an example of creating and using a framebuffer in OpenGL:

```
GLuint framebuffer;

glGenFramebuffers(1, &framebuffer);

glBindFramebuffer(GL_FRAMEBUFFER, framebuffer);

// Create and attach a texture for color rendering

GLuint textureColor;

glGenTextures(1, &textureColor);

glBindTexture(GL_TEXTURE_2D, textureColor);

glTexImage2D(GL_TEXTURE_2D, 0, GL_RGB, screenWidth, screenHeight, 0, GL_RGB, GL_UNSIGNED_BYTE, NULL);

glFramebufferTexture2D(GL_FRAMEBUFFER, GL_COLOR_ATTACHMENT0, GL_TEXTURE_2D, textureColor, 0);

// Create and attach a renderbuffer for depth and stencil rendering

GLuint renderbufferDepthStencil;

glGenRenderbuffers(1, &renderbufferDepthStencil);
```

```
glBindRenderbuffer(GL_RENDERBUFFER, renderbufferDepthStencil);

glRenderbufferStorage(GL_RENDERBUFFER, GL_DEPTH24_STENCIL8, screenWidth, screenHeight);

glFramebufferRenderbuffer(GL_FRAMEBUFFER, GL_DEPTH_STENCIL_ATTACHMENT, GL_RENDERBUFFER, renderbufferDepthStencil);

// Check framebuffer completeness

if (glCheckFramebufferStatus(GL_FRAMEBUFFER) != GL_FRAMEBUFFER_COMPLETE) {

// Handle framebuffer error

}

// Rendering to the framebuffer

glBindFramebuffer(GL_FRAMEBUFFER, framebuffer);

// Perform rendering passes here

// Return to the default framebuffer (the screen)

glBindFramebuffer(GL_FRAMEBUFFER, 0);
```

In this example, we create a framebuffer, attach a color texture, and a depth-stencil renderbuffer. After setting up the framebuffer, we can render the scene to it, apply post-processing effects, and combine multiple passes to achieve advanced rendering results.

Multi-Pass Rendering

Multi-pass rendering involves rendering a scene in multiple steps or passes to achieve complex visual effects. Each pass can apply different shaders, techniques, or modifications to the scene. Common use cases for multi-pass rendering include applying post-processing effects like bloom, motion blur, and depth of field.

Here's a simplified example of multi-pass rendering in OpenGL:

// First pass: Render the scene to a framebuffer

glBindFramebuffer(GL_FRAMEBUFFER, framebuffer);

// Render the scene using a basic shader

// Second pass: Apply post-processing effects

glBindFramebuffer(GL_FRAMEBUFFER,
postProcessingFramebuffer);

// Use a post-processing shader to modify the scene

In this example, the first pass renders the scene to a framebuffer, and the second pass applies post-processing effects by rendering the framebuffer's texture to another framebuffer with a post-processing shader. This separation allows for the application of various effects without modifying the original scene.

Post-Processing Effects

Post-processing effects are techniques applied to the rendered image after the scene has been rendered to achieve specific visual enhancements. These effects can greatly improve the quality and realism of graphics in real-time applications.

Common post-processing effects include:

- **Bloom:** Adds a glowing effect to bright areas in the scene.

- **Motion Blur:** Simulates motion blur for fast-moving objects.

- **Depth of Field:** Creates a realistic depth-based blurring effect.

- **HDR (High Dynamic Range):** Enhances the contrast and brightness range of the scene.

- **Ambient Occlusion:** Adds shading to concave areas, improving realism.

To implement post-processing effects, you'll typically use a framebuffer to render the scene to a texture, apply the effect in a shader, and then render the texture to the screen. The specific implementation details can vary depending on the effect.

In the upcoming sections, we will explore each of these advanced OpenGL rendering techniques in more detail, providing code examples and practical insights to help you incorporate them into your graphics programming projects.

Section 12.3: Advanced WebGL Rendering Techniques

In this section, we will delve into advanced WebGL rendering techniques that go beyond the basics discussed in earlier chapters. These techniques are essential for achieving stunning and interactive 3D graphics in web applications. We'll cover topics such as deferred shading, environment mapping, and advanced shader effects.

Deferred Shading

Deferred shading is a rendering technique that improves performance by separating the lighting calculations from the geometry rendering. Instead of calculating lighting for each pixel during the rendering pass, deferred shading stores various properties (such as position, normal, and material properties) in separate buffers. Later, a lighting pass is performed to compute the final pixel colors based on the stored information.

Implementing deferred shading in WebGL involves several steps:

1. **Geometry Pass:** Render the scene to multiple render targets (framebuffers) to store information about each pixel, including position, normal, and material properties.
2. **Lighting Pass:** Use the information from the geometry pass to calculate lighting contributions from various light sources. This often involves complex shader programs.
3. **Combine Pass:** Combine the results of the lighting pass with the original colors to produce the final image.

Here's a simplified example of deferred shading in WebGL:

```
// Geometry Pass

// Render scene to multiple textures (G-buffer)

bindGeometryFramebuffer();

clear();

renderGeometry();

// Lighting Pass

bindLightingFramebuffer();
```

```
clear();

for (let light of lights) {

// Use the G-buffer textures and light properties to calculate lighting

renderLighting(light);

}

// Combine Pass

bindDefaultFramebuffer();

clear();

combineResults();
```

Deferred shading can significantly improve the performance of WebGL applications, especially when there are multiple light sources or complex materials.

Environment Mapping

Environment mapping is a technique used to simulate reflections and refractions on surfaces by using cube maps or spherical maps. It allows for realistic rendering of materials that interact with their surroundings, such as mirrors or glass.

To implement environment mapping in WebGL, you'll typically use cube maps, which consist of six textures representing the environment from different directions (up, down, left, right, front, back). You sample these cube maps in shaders to calculate the reflection or refraction vector for each pixel.

Here's a high-level overview of environment mapping in WebGL:

1. **Cube Map Generation:** Create cube maps representing the environment or the scene from different viewpoints.
2. **Rendering Pass:** Render the reflective or refractive object, sampling the cube map to calculate the reflection or refraction vector for each pixel.
3. **Shader Calculation:** In the shader, use the reflection or refraction vector to sample the cube map and determine the final color of the pixel.

Environment mapping is particularly useful for achieving realistic material effects in WebGL, adding a level of visual fidelity to your 3D scenes.

Advanced Shader Effects

WebGL allows you to create complex shader effects to achieve various visual enhancements. These effects include:

- **Screen Space Reflections (SSR):** Simulates reflections based on the screen-space information, improving the realism of water and reflective surfaces.

- **Volumetric Rendering:** Renders realistic fog, smoke, or atmospheric effects by simulating the scattering of light within a volume.

- **Toon Shading:** Creates a stylized, cel-shaded look for your 3D models, often seen in animation or comic-style games.

- **GPU Particle Systems:** Simulate and render thousands of particles efficiently on the GPU for effects like fire, smoke, or sparks.

To implement these advanced shader effects, you'll need a good understanding of GLSL (OpenGL Shading Language) and WebGL. Writing custom shaders and managing resources like textures and framebuffers are common tasks in achieving these effects.

In the upcoming sections, we will dive deeper into each of these advanced WebGL rendering techniques, providing code examples and practical guidance to help you incorporate them into your web-based 3D graphics projects.

Section 12.4: Real-Time Rendering in WebGL

Real-time rendering is a crucial aspect of modern 3D graphics, and WebGL plays a significant role in enabling interactive and visually stunning experiences on the web. In this section, we will explore the principles and techniques behind real-time rendering in WebGL, focusing on how to achieve high-performance rendering for interactive web applications.

The Importance of Real-Time Rendering

Real-time rendering refers to the ability to generate and display images at interactive frame rates, typically 30 frames per second (FPS) or higher. Achieving real-time rendering is vital for various applications, including video games, simulations, architectural visualization, and more. It ensures that the graphics respond quickly to user input, creating an immersive and engaging experience.

WebGL Optimization for Real-Time Rendering

To achieve real-time rendering in WebGL, you need to optimize various aspects of your graphics pipeline. Here are some key considerations:

1. **Shader Efficiency:** Write efficient GLSL shaders that minimize redundant calculations and use GPU resources effectively. Avoid complex computations that can slow down rendering.
2. **Mesh Optimization:** Use techniques like level-of-detail (LOD) models or mesh simplification to reduce the polygon count of 3D models. This helps maintain a high frame rate, especially in complex scenes.
3. **Texture Compression:** Compress textures to reduce memory usage and improve texture streaming performance. WebGL supports various texture compression formats like DXT and ETC.
4. **Batching and Instancing:** Combine multiple objects with the same material and shader into a single draw call whenever possible. Instancing allows you to render multiple instances of the same object efficiently.
5. **Culling Techniques:** Implement view frustum culling and occlusion culling to avoid rendering objects that are not visible to the camera. This reduces unnecessary rendering computations.
6. **Asynchronous Loading:** Use asynchronous techniques to load assets like textures and models. This ensures that the loading process doesn't block the main rendering loop.
7. **Frame Buffer Management:** Be mindful of framebuffer operations. Minimize the number of render-to-texture passes if they are not necessary for your rendering effects.
8. **Shader Effects:** Balance the use of shader effects and post-processing. Some effects may be computationally expensive and affect real-time performance.

Real-Time Rendering Challenges

Real-time rendering in WebGL also comes with its set of challenges. Here are a few common ones:

- **Cross-Browser Compatibility:** WebGL performance can vary across different browsers and platforms. Testing and optimizing for various environments is essential.

- **Mobile Devices:** Ensuring smooth rendering on mobile devices with limited GPU power requires additional optimization and consideration of mobile-specific rendering techniques.

- **Dynamic Lighting:** Real-time rendering of dynamic lighting and shadows can be computationally intensive. Techniques like shadow mapping and screen space reflections may be needed.

- **Texture Memory:** Managing texture memory is critical. Loading high-resolution textures can consume significant GPU memory, impacting performance.

- **WebGL API Limitations:** WebGL has some limitations compared to native graphics APIs, so achieving certain advanced rendering effects may be challenging.

In summary, real-time rendering in WebGL is achievable with careful optimization and an understanding of the principles involved. It involves a balance between visual fidelity and performance, making it an exciting field for web-based 3D graphics developers. In the following sections, we will explore practical examples and tips to help you achieve real-time rendering excellence in your WebGL projects.

Section 12.5: Comparative Analysis of Rendering Capabilities

In this section, we'll conduct a comparative analysis of rendering capabilities between WebGL and native OpenGL. Both WebGL and native OpenGL are powerful graphics APIs, but they have some key differences and trade-offs in terms of rendering capabilities.

WebGL Rendering Capabilities

WebGL is designed to bring 3D graphics to the web, making it accessible to a wide audience. However, due to its web-based nature, it has certain limitations:

1. **Performance:** WebGL performance heavily depends on the user's hardware and the browser being used. High-quality rendering may not be achievable on all devices, especially older ones.
2. **Cross-Browser Variability:** Different browsers may have varying levels of WebGL support and performance. Developers need to consider cross-browser compatibility and potentially write browser-specific code for optimal performance.
3. **Security Restrictions:** WebGL runs in a sandboxed environment for security reasons. This limits access to certain features that might be available in native OpenGL.
4. **Resource Constraints:** WebGL applications must operate within the constraints of the web environment. This includes limitations on memory usage and file access, which can affect the rendering capabilities.

5. **Shader Precision:** WebGL shaders are subject to shader precision constraints, which can affect the accuracy of certain rendering calculations, particularly in complex shaders.
6. **Texture Compression:** WebGL supports texture compression but has fewer texture formats available compared to native OpenGL.
7. **Limited Access to Hardware:** WebGL has limited access to hardware features, which can impact rendering performance and flexibility compared to native OpenGL.

Despite these limitations, WebGL is a versatile technology that allows developers to create impressive 3D graphics and simulations that run directly in web browsers without the need for plugins.

Native OpenGL Rendering Capabilities

Native OpenGL, on the other hand, offers more flexibility and control over rendering capabilities:

1. **Direct Hardware Access:** Native OpenGL provides direct access to the underlying GPU hardware, enabling fine-grained control over rendering operations. This results in potentially higher performance and more rendering capabilities.
2. **Full Shader Precision:** In native OpenGL, shader precision is typically not limited, allowing for more accurate rendering calculations.
3. **Extensive Texture Formats:** Native OpenGL supports a wide range of texture formats, including compressed textures, giving developers more options for optimizing memory usage.
4. **Custom Rendering Pipelines:** With native OpenGL, you

can implement custom rendering pipelines tailored to your specific needs, whereas WebGL adheres to a fixed pipeline model.

5. **Access to GPU Features:** Native OpenGL allows access to advanced GPU features and extensions, enabling the implementation of cutting-edge rendering techniques.

However, using native OpenGL also comes with challenges, such as platform-specific development and deployment, which can be more complex compared to WebGL's web-based deployment model.

Choosing Between WebGL and Native OpenGL

The choice between WebGL and native OpenGL depends on your project's requirements and target audience. If you aim to create web-based applications that reach a broad user base, WebGL is an excellent choice. It offers portability and ease of deployment.

On the other hand, if you're developing desktop applications or games that require maximum performance and you have control over the target hardware and platform, native OpenGL provides greater rendering capabilities and flexibility.

In many cases, developers leverage both technologies. They may develop core rendering logic in native OpenGL and then create WebGL-based versions for web deployment, ensuring a wider reach while taking advantage of the full rendering capabilities of native OpenGL where available.

In conclusion, both WebGL and native OpenGL have their strengths and weaknesses, and the choice between them should be based on your project's specific needs and constraints. Understanding the differences and capabilities of each technology is crucial for making informed decisions in graphics programming.

Chapter 13: Mobile Graphics with WebGL

Section 13.1: Overview of Mobile Graphics

Mobile devices have become an integral part of our daily lives, and their graphics capabilities have advanced significantly over the years. In this section, we'll explore the world of mobile graphics with a focus on WebGL and its adaptation for mobile devices.

The Mobile Graphics Landscape

Mobile devices, including smartphones and tablets, are equipped with powerful GPUs (Graphics Processing Units) that enable impressive graphics rendering. The mobile graphics landscape is diverse, with various platforms, operating systems, and hardware configurations. Some key points to consider:

- **iOS and Android:** The two dominant mobile operating systems, iOS (Apple) and Android (Google), have their own graphics APIs and development environments. iOS primarily uses Metal, while Android uses Vulkan and OpenGL ES.

- **Graphics APIs:** OpenGL ES (OpenGL for Embedded Systems) is a widely adopted graphics API for mobile devices, offering a standardized way to access GPU capabilities. WebGL, being based on OpenGL ES, provides compatibility between web and mobile graphics.

- **Hardware Variability:** Mobile devices come in various hardware configurations, including different GPU vendors, memory sizes, and screen resolutions.

Developers need to consider these variations for optimal performance and compatibility.

Adapting WebGL for Mobile Devices

WebGL is a versatile technology for creating 3D graphics on the web, and it can also be adapted for mobile devices. Here are some key considerations when working with WebGL on mobile:

1. **Performance Optimization:** Mobile devices often have resource constraints compared to desktop computers. To ensure smooth performance, optimize your WebGL applications by minimizing memory usage, reducing the complexity of shaders, and optimizing rendering pipelines.
2. **Touch Interaction:** Mobile devices rely on touch input for user interaction. Implement touch controls and gestures to make your WebGL applications mobile-friendly. Consider providing both touch and mouse/keyboard controls for cross-platform support.
3. **Viewport and Resolution:** Adapt your WebGL application to different screen resolutions and aspect ratios. Use responsive design techniques to ensure your graphics look good on a variety of mobile devices.
4. **Orientation Support:** Mobile devices can be used in both portrait and landscape orientations. Handle orientation changes gracefully, adjusting the camera and UI layout as needed.
5. **Battery Life Considerations:** Graphics-intensive applications can consume significant battery power. Optimize rendering to minimize power consumption and provide user options to adjust quality settings for better battery life.
6. **Cross-Platform Compatibility:** WebGL applications

designed for mobile should also consider cross-browser compatibility. Test your applications on different mobile browsers to ensure a consistent user experience.

7. **WebGL 2.0:** WebGL 2.0 introduces several improvements over WebGL 1.0, including better performance and additional features. Check for WebGL 2.0 support on target mobile devices and consider using its capabilities if available.

Case Studies: Mobile Applications Using WebGL

Mobile graphics with WebGL have found applications in various domains, including gaming, education, simulations, and virtual tours. Some examples include:

- **Mobile Games:** Many mobile games use WebGL for rendering 3D graphics, providing console-like experiences on smartphones and tablets.

- **Educational Apps:** WebGL is used in educational applications to create interactive 3D models and simulations for learning purposes.

- **Virtual Tours:** Real estate and tourism apps often incorporate WebGL to offer virtual tours of properties and destinations.

- **Medical Simulations:** WebGL is utilized in medical applications for interactive 3D visualizations and simulations.

- **Augmented Reality:** Some augmented reality (AR) applications use WebGL for rendering virtual objects in the real world.

Conclusion

Mobile graphics with WebGL open up exciting possibilities for developers to create engaging and interactive applications for a broad audience. However, developing for mobile devices comes with its unique challenges and considerations, including performance optimization, touch interaction, and cross-platform compatibility. Understanding the mobile graphics landscape and adapting WebGL-based applications accordingly can lead to successful and visually impressive mobile experiences.

Section 13.2: Adapting WebGL for Mobile Devices

Adapting WebGL for mobile devices is a crucial aspect of developing graphics applications that target smartphones and tablets. In this section, we'll explore the strategies and best practices for optimizing WebGL content to ensure a smooth and responsive experience on mobile.

Performance Optimization

1. **Shader Complexity:** Mobile GPUs may not handle complex shaders as efficiently as desktop GPUs. Optimize your shaders to reduce the number of instructions and texture fetches. Consider using simpler shading models and techniques when possible.
2. **Texture Compression:** Use texture compression formats like ETC2 (Ericsson Texture Compression) or ASTC (Adaptive Scalable Texture Compression) to reduce texture memory consumption and bandwidth usage while maintaining visual quality.
3. **Mipmapping:** Implement mipmapping for textures to

improve texture sampling performance, especially when objects are at varying distances from the camera. Mipmaps provide pre-scaled versions of textures for different levels of detail.

4. **Geometry Optimization:** Minimize the number of vertices in your 3D models and use level-of-detail (LOD) techniques to reduce the geometric complexity of distant objects.
5. **Frame Rate Control:** Limit the frame rate for your application to conserve battery life and prevent overheating on mobile devices. Implement a dynamic frame rate control mechanism that adjusts based on the device's performance capabilities.

Touch Interaction

1. **Touch Controls:** Design intuitive touch controls and gestures for user interaction. Implement common gestures like pinch-to-zoom, swipe, and tap. Ensure that touch controls are responsive and provide feedback to users.
2. **Multi-Touch Support:** Take advantage of multi-touch capabilities on modern mobile devices. Support interactions involving multiple fingers, such as two-finger rotation or three-finger gestures.
3. **Virtual Joysticks:** For games or applications that require precise control, consider using virtual joysticks or on-screen buttons. These elements can enhance the user experience, especially in gaming apps.
4. **Testing on Real Devices:** Test touch interactions on a variety of real mobile devices to ensure compatibility and responsiveness. Emulators may not always accurately represent real touch behavior.

Responsive Design

1. **Viewport and Aspect Ratio:** Create a responsive design that adapts to different screen sizes and aspect ratios. Use CSS media queries to adjust the canvas size and layout based on the device's screen dimensions.
2. **Orientation Handling:** Handle changes in device orientation (portrait and landscape) gracefully. Adjust the camera settings and UI layout to accommodate both orientations.
3. **Retina and High-DPI Displays:** Account for high-DPI (dots per inch) displays commonly found in modern mobile devices. Use devicePixelRatio to scale your WebGL content appropriately for these displays.

Battery Life Considerations

1. **Power-Efficient Rendering:** Implement power-efficient rendering techniques, such as reducing the rendering workload when the application is in the background or not in use.
2. **User-Controlled Quality:** Allow users to adjust graphics quality settings in your application. This can help conserve battery life by allowing users to trade off visual fidelity for longer usage.
3. **Battery Monitoring:** Monitor battery levels and provide notifications or options for users to save battery when their device is running low.

Cross-Platform Compatibility

1. **Browser Compatibility:** Test your WebGL application on various mobile web browsers (Safari, Chrome, Firefox, etc.)

to ensure it works consistently across different platforms. Be aware of browser-specific quirks and limitations.

2. **WebGL 2.0 Consideration:** If your application targets newer mobile devices, consider taking advantage of WebGL 2.0 features for improved performance and capabilities.

Case Studies

Several successful mobile applications leverage WebGL for graphics rendering:

- **Mobile Games:** Many popular mobile games, including 3D action, puzzle, and simulation games, use WebGL to deliver immersive gaming experiences on smartphones and tablets.

- **Educational Apps:** Educational applications on mobile platforms use WebGL to create interactive 3D models and simulations for learning purposes, enhancing engagement and understanding.

- **Virtual Tours:** Real estate and tourism apps offer virtual tours of properties and destinations, allowing users to explore and interact with 3D environments.

- **Medical Simulations:** WebGL is employed in medical applications to visualize complex 3D models, enabling interactive simulations and surgical planning on mobile devices.

- **Augmented Reality:** Some augmented reality (AR) apps use WebGL for rendering virtual objects in the real world, enhancing the AR experience with 3D graphics.

Conclusion

Adapting WebGL content for mobile devices involves a combination of performance optimization, touch interaction design, responsive layout considerations, battery life management, and cross-browser compatibility testing. By following best practices and considering the unique characteristics of mobile hardware, you can create engaging and responsive WebGL applications that cater to a wide mobile audience. Mobile WebGL applications continue to push the boundaries of what's possible in mobile graphics, making them a valuable addition to various domains, from gaming to education and beyond.

Section 13.3: Performance Optimization on Mobile

Performance optimization is a critical aspect of developing WebGL applications for mobile devices. To ensure smooth and responsive experiences on smartphones and tablets, developers need to pay close attention to performance considerations. In this section, we'll explore various strategies and techniques for optimizing WebGL content on mobile platforms.

1. Minimize Draw Calls

Reducing the number of draw calls is a fundamental optimization technique. Each draw call incurs CPU overhead, so it's essential to batch as many objects as possible into a single draw call. Use techniques like instanced rendering, where multiple instances of an object are rendered with a single draw call, to improve efficiency.

```
// Example of using instanced rendering in WebGL

gl.drawArraysInstanced(mode, first, count, instanceCount);
```

2. Efficient Shader Programs

Mobile GPUs have limitations compared to desktop counterparts. Use simpler shader programs whenever possible. Avoid unnecessary branching and calculations. Implement conditional logic in shaders efficiently to minimize performance impact.

3. Texture Optimization

Texture memory can be a bottleneck on mobile devices. Optimize textures by using compression formats like ETC2 or ASTC. Use texture atlases to reduce the number of texture switches. Implement texture streaming to load and unload textures dynamically based on proximity to the camera.

```
// Texture atlas example in WebGL

gl.activeTexture(gl.TEXTURE0);

gl.bindTexture(gl.TEXTURE_2D, atlasTexture);

gl.uniform1i(uSampler, 0);
```

4. Level of Detail (LOD)

Implement LOD techniques for 3D models to reduce geometric complexity for objects at a distance. Use lower-polygon versions of models or decrease the level of detail dynamically based on the object's screen size. This reduces CPU and GPU load.

5. Dynamic Batching

Implement dynamic batching for objects that share the same shader and material properties. This technique combines multiple objects into a single vertex buffer, reducing draw calls and improving performance.

```
// Dynamic batching example in WebGL
const mergedVertices = mergeObjects(objects);
gl.bufferData(gl.ARRAY_BUFFER, mergedVertices, gl.STATIC_DRAW);
```

6. Texture Compression

Use texture compression formats like PVRTC or DXT on platforms that support them. Compressed textures reduce memory usage and improve loading times.

7. GPU Profiling

Use GPU profiling tools provided by browser developer tools to identify performance bottlenecks. Profiling helps pinpoint areas that need optimization, such as expensive shaders or excessive texture uploads.

8. Asynchronous Operations

Offload non-critical operations to worker threads or use asynchronous programming techniques to prevent the main thread from becoming blocked. This ensures that the application remains responsive to user input.

9. Culling and Occlusion

Implement frustum culling to avoid rendering objects outside the camera's view frustum. Additionally, use occlusion culling techniques to skip rendering objects hidden behind others.

10. Mobile-Specific Features

Leverage mobile-specific features, such as hardware acceleration for specific tasks. For example, use WebGL's WEBGL_compressed_texture_astc extension for ASTC texture compression if supported.

```
// Example of using ASTC texture compression extension

const astcExt = gl.getExtension('WEBGL_compressed_texture_astc');

if (astcExt) {

// Use ASTC texture compression

}
```

11. Test on Real Devices

Always test your WebGL application on a variety of real mobile devices to ensure compatibility and performance. Emulators may not accurately represent the performance characteristics of actual devices.

12. User-Controlled Quality

Allow users to adjust graphics quality settings within your application. Providing options to reduce visual fidelity can help users with older or less powerful devices enjoy your content without performance issues.

Optimizing WebGL performance on mobile devices requires a combination of careful planning, profiling, and implementation of performance-enhancing techniques. By following these best practices, you can deliver a smoother and more enjoyable experience to mobile users while making the most of the hardware capabilities available on their devices.

Section 13.4: Touch Interaction and Mobile-Specific Features

Developing WebGL applications for mobile devices involves adapting to touch input and leveraging mobile-specific features to enhance user experiences. In this section, we will explore touch interaction techniques and mobile-specific features that can be integrated into your WebGL applications.

1. Touch Input Handling

Mobile devices primarily rely on touch input for user interaction. WebGL applications should be designed to respond to touch gestures, such as taps, swipes, and pinch-to-zoom. You can use JavaScript event listeners to capture touch events and translate them into interactions within your application.

```
// Example of handling a tap event in WebGL

canvas.addEventListener('touchstart', function(event) {

const touchX = event.touches[0].clientX;

const touchY = event.touches[0].clientY;

// Perform actions based on touch coordinates

}, false);
```

2. Gestures and Multi-Touch

Implementing gestures like rotation and scaling can enhance user interactions with 3D models or scenes. Libraries like Hammer.js can simplify the handling of multi-touch gestures in WebGL applications.

```
// Example of using Hammer.js for pinch and rotate gestures

const hammertime = new Hammer(canvas);

hammertime.get('pinch').set({ enable: true });

hammertime.get('rotate').set({ enable: true });

hammertime.on('pinch', function(event) {

const scale = event.scale;

// Perform scaling based on pinch gesture

});

hammertime.on('rotate', function(event) {

const rotation = event.rotation;

// Perform rotation based on rotate gesture

});
```

3. Device Orientation

Mobile devices often have built-in sensors like accelerometers and gyroscopes. You can use the deviceorientation event to access the device's orientation data and use it to control the camera or objects in your WebGL scene.

```
// Example of using device orientation data in WebGL

window.addEventListener('deviceorientation', function(event) {

const alpha = event.alpha; // Z-axis rotation
```

```
const beta = event.beta; // X-axis rotation

const gamma = event.gamma; // Y-axis rotation

// Adjust camera or object orientation based on device data

});
```

4. Fullscreen Mode

Mobile users expect a fullscreen experience. You can use the Fullscreen API to allow users to enter fullscreen mode, providing a more immersive experience for WebGL applications.

```
// Example of toggling fullscreen mode in WebGL

const canvas = document.getElementById('webgl-canvas');

canvas.addEventListener('click', function() {

if (canvas.requestFullscreen) {

canvas.requestFullscreen();

} else if (canvas.mozRequestFullScreen) {

canvas.mozRequestFullScreen();

} else if (canvas.webkitRequestFullscreen) {

canvas.webkitRequestFullscreen();

}

});
```

5. Mobile-Specific Features

Consider integrating mobile-specific features like device vibration, geolocation, and access to the device's camera. These features can be used creatively to enhance interactivity and engagement in your WebGL applications.

```
// Example of using the device's vibration feature

if (navigator.vibrate) {

// Vibrate for 500 milliseconds

navigator.vibrate(500);

}
```

6. Responsive Design

Ensure that your WebGL application has a responsive design that adapts to various screen sizes and orientations. Use CSS media queries to adjust layout and content based on the device's characteristics.

```
/* Example of a media query for responsive design */

@media (max-width: 768px) {

/* Adjust styles for smaller screens */

}
```

7. Performance Considerations

Mobile devices have limited resources compared to desktop computers. Keep performance in mind when implementing touch interactions and mobile-specific features. Optimize code and minimize unnecessary computations to ensure a smooth experience.

In summary, designing WebGL applications for mobile devices involves accommodating touch input, implementing gestures, utilizing device orientation, and making the most of mobile-specific features. By considering these aspects and providing a seamless and engaging mobile experience, you can create WebGL applications that resonate with a broader audience and deliver a compelling user experience on smartphones and tablets.

Section 13.5: Case Studies: Mobile Applications Using WebGL

In this section, we'll explore several case studies of real-world mobile applications that leverage WebGL to deliver immersive and interactive experiences. These examples demonstrate the versatility and potential of WebGL in the mobile app development landscape.

1. Google Maps

Google Maps is one of the most popular navigation apps, and it utilizes WebGL extensively for rendering interactive maps and satellite imagery. WebGL enables smooth panning, zooming, and rotating of maps, providing users with a seamless and responsive mapping experience on their mobile devices. The use of 3D buildings and terrain features also adds to the realism of the maps.

2. Sketchfab

Sketchfab is a platform for sharing and viewing 3D models. Their mobile app utilizes WebGL to display detailed 3D models interactively. Users can explore and manipulate 3D models by rotating, zooming, and panning, all powered by WebGL, making it an excellent tool for 3D artists and enthusiasts on the go.

3. IKEA Place

IKEA Place is an augmented reality (AR) app that allows users to place virtual furniture in their real-world surroundings using their smartphone's camera. WebGL is used to render realistic 3D models of IKEA furniture within the app. This provides users with a true-to-scale preview of how furniture will look and fit in their homes before making a purchase.

4. Framer

Framer is a design and prototyping tool that helps designers create interactive prototypes. The Framer mobile app leverages WebGL to display and interact with complex design prototypes seamlessly on mobile devices. Designers can test and showcase their interactive designs on smartphones and tablets.

5. PlayCanvas

PlayCanvas is a game engine that utilizes WebGL for creating and running real-time 3D games directly in web browsers, including on mobile devices. The PlayCanvas mobile app allows users to play WebGL-powered games on their smartphones, demonstrating the potential of WebGL for mobile gaming.

6. Babylon.js Viewer

Babylon.js is a JavaScript framework for building 3D experiences on the web. The Babylon.js Viewer app for mobile devices showcases 3D scenes and models created with the framework. Users can interact with 3D content and explore its features on their smartphones and tablets.

7. Three.js Editor

Three.js is a popular 3D graphics library for the web, and the Three.js Editor app extends its capabilities to mobile devices. It allows users to create, edit, and view 3D scenes and models on their smartphones, demonstrating the portability of WebGL-powered 3D content creation.

8. Simulations and Education Apps

Many educational apps and simulations use WebGL to provide interactive learning experiences on mobile devices. Examples include chemistry simulations, astronomy apps, and virtual tours of historical sites. WebGL enables these apps to offer engaging and immersive educational content.

These case studies illustrate how WebGL has been adopted across various domains in mobile app development. From navigation and design to gaming and education, WebGL empowers developers to create captivating and interactive experiences for mobile users. As mobile devices continue to advance in terms of performance and graphics capabilities, the role of WebGL in mobile app development is likely to expand further, offering users richer and more engaging experiences.

Chapter 14: Virtual and Augmented Reality

Section 14.1: Basics of VR and AR

Virtual Reality (VR) and Augmented Reality (AR) are transformative technologies that blend the digital and physical worlds to create immersive experiences. In this section, we'll delve into the fundamental concepts of VR and AR, exploring what sets them apart and how they are shaping the future of graphics programming.

Understanding Virtual Reality (VR)

Virtual Reality is a technology that immerses users in a completely digital environment, often by using a head-mounted display (HMD) and motion-tracking sensors. The goal of VR is to transport users to a computer-generated world that can be entirely fictional or a realistic simulation of the real world. VR applications can range from gaming and entertainment to training simulations and medical applications.

Key characteristics of VR include:

- **Immersive Environment:** VR aims to create a sense of presence, making users feel like they are physically present in the digital environment. This is achieved through a combination of 3D graphics, spatial audio, and responsive interactions.

- **Head Tracking:** VR systems track the user's head movements in real-time, adjusting the view accordingly. This allows users to look around and explore the virtual world as they would in the real world.

- **Motion Controllers:** Many VR setups include handheld controllers that enable users to interact with objects and perform actions within the virtual environment. These controllers are often tracked in 3D space.

- **Spatial Audio:** Realistic audio is crucial in VR to provide an accurate sense of direction and distance for sounds within the virtual environment. This enhances immersion and spatial awareness.

- **Full Stereoscopic 3D:** VR displays present a slightly different image to each eye, creating a stereoscopic 3D effect. This depth perception contributes to the feeling of immersion.

Exploring Augmented Reality (AR)

Augmented Reality, on the other hand, blends digital content with the real world. Instead of replacing the physical environment, AR enhances it by overlaying digital information onto the user's view of the real world. AR experiences are typically viewed through a smartphone or AR glasses.

Key characteristics of AR include:

- **Real-World Integration:** AR applications must seamlessly integrate digital content with the user's surroundings. This involves real-time tracking of the physical environment and objects.

- **Mobile Devices:** AR experiences are often delivered through smartphones or tablets, which have cameras and sensors to perceive the real world. AR apps can overlay information, such as directions, product details, or gaming elements, onto the device's screen.

- **Marker-Based and Markerless Tracking:** AR can use markers (visual cues) or markerless techniques (like SLAM - Simultaneous Localization and Mapping) to understand the user's environment. Markerless AR is particularly versatile as it doesn't rely on predefined markers.

- **Interactivity:** AR encourages users to interact with the real world while engaging with digital content. This interaction can involve tapping on the screen, scanning objects, or using gestures.

- **Practical Applications:** AR has applications in various fields, including navigation (e.g., AR navigation apps), education (e.g., interactive textbooks), marketing (e.g., AR product catalogs), and industrial use (e.g., maintenance and assembly instructions).

It's important to note that VR and AR are not mutually exclusive. Mixed Reality (MR) represents a spectrum that combines aspects of both VR and AR. MR systems, like Microsoft HoloLens, allow users to interact with both digital and physical elements simultaneously, creating compelling hybrid experiences.

In the following sections, we'll explore how these technologies can be implemented and leveraged in OpenGL and WebGL, opening up new possibilities for graphics programming in VR and AR contexts.

Section 14.2: Implementing VR in OpenGL

Virtual Reality (VR) has gained immense popularity for its ability to provide immersive experiences. To implement VR in OpenGL, you'll need to understand the essential concepts and components involved. In this section, we'll explore the key steps to implement VR functionality using OpenGL.

VR Hardware

Before diving into implementation, it's crucial to choose the right VR hardware for your project. Some popular VR hardware options include the Oculus Rift, HTC Vive, and Valve Index. These systems typically consist of a headset with a screen, motion-tracking sensors, and motion controllers. Make sure to select hardware that aligns with your application's requirements and target audience.

VR Rendering Pipeline

VR rendering involves creating two slightly different views—one for each eye—to achieve a stereoscopic effect. The following steps outline the typical VR rendering pipeline:

1. **Initialization:** Initialize the VR hardware and create OpenGL contexts for each eye.
2. **Eye Rendering:** Render the scene from the perspective of each eye. This involves setting up the camera for the left and right eyes and rendering the scene separately. Keep in mind that the camera parameters (e.g., field of view and projection matrices) may differ for each eye.
3. **Distortion Correction:** Apply lens distortion correction to the rendered images to account for the optics of the VR headset. This step ensures that the final image appears undistorted when viewed through the VR headset's lenses.

4. **Combining Views:** Combine the left and right eye views into a single stereo image. This can be done by simply placing them side by side or by using specific texture formats designed for VR.
5. **Display:** Display the combined stereo image on the VR headset's screens. The hardware takes care of displaying the images correctly to each eye, considering the headset's optics.

VR Interaction

Interaction is a crucial aspect of VR applications. Users should be able to interact with objects and navigate through the virtual environment. This can be achieved through motion controllers or other input devices provided by the VR hardware.

In OpenGL, you'll need to handle input from motion controllers or other devices and use it to manipulate objects or trigger actions within your VR scene. This may involve updating the position and orientation of objects based on controller input and implementing collision detection for interactions.

VR Best Practices

Here are some best practices to keep in mind when implementing VR in OpenGL:

- **Optimization:** VR applications require high frame rates to avoid motion sickness. Optimize your rendering pipeline, use efficient shaders, and reduce unnecessary rendering to maintain a smooth experience.

- **Comfort:** Minimize any factors that can cause discomfort, such as latency, judder, or excessive head movement. These issues can lead to motion sickness, which is a common concern in VR.

- **User Interface (UI):** Design user interfaces that are comfortable and easy to navigate in VR. Consider how users will interact with menus, buttons, and other UI elements within the virtual environment.

- **Performance:** Monitor and optimize performance continuously. VR applications demand a lot from the hardware, so efficient rendering and minimal latency are critical.

- **Testing:** Extensive testing is essential to ensure that the VR experience is comfortable and free from issues. Test on different VR hardware if possible to ensure compatibility.

Implementing VR in OpenGL opens up exciting possibilities for creating immersive applications, whether for gaming, simulations, or other interactive experiences. However, it requires careful consideration of hardware, rendering techniques, interaction design, and performance optimization to deliver a compelling VR experience.

Section 14.3: Implementing VR and AR in WebGL

Virtual Reality (VR) and Augmented Reality (AR) have gained significant attention for their ability to provide immersive and interactive experiences. Implementing VR and AR in WebGL enables developers to create web-based applications that leverage these technologies, making them accessible across a wide range of devices. In this section, we'll explore the key concepts and steps involved in implementing VR and AR in WebGL.

VR and AR in the Browser

WebGL, the web's graphics language, allows developers to create 3D graphics and interactive experiences within a web browser. To implement VR and AR in WebGL, you can leverage various libraries and APIs that provide support for these technologies.

WebXR API

The WebXR API is a standard that enables VR and AR experiences in web browsers. It provides a set of JavaScript functions and interfaces for creating immersive experiences. To use WebXR, you'll need a compatible web browser and a device that supports VR or AR, such as VR headsets or AR-enabled smartphones.

Here's a high-level overview of the steps to implement VR and AR using the WebXR API in WebGL:

1. **Initialization:** Initialize the WebXR API and request access to VR or AR devices. This step ensures that the user's hardware is ready for immersive experiences.
2. **Session Creation:** Create an XR session, which represents the user's presence in a VR or AR environment. This session manages the rendering loop and interaction events.
3. **Rendering:** Use WebGL to render your 3D scene within the XR session. The rendering process involves creating separate views for each eye in VR or overlaying virtual objects onto the real world in AR.
4. **Interaction:** Implement user interactions using input sources provided by the XR session. This can include

controller input in VR or gesture recognition in AR.

5. **Session Termination:** Properly end the XR session when the user exits the VR or AR experience.

A-Frame Framework

A-Frame is a popular framework for building VR and AR experiences on the web. It simplifies the development process by providing a declarative markup language for creating 3D scenes in HTML. A-Frame is built on top of WebGL and WebXR, making it an accessible choice for web developers.

Design Considerations

When implementing VR and AR in WebGL, consider the following design considerations:

- **Performance:** VR and AR experiences demand high performance to maintain a smooth frame rate. Optimize your WebGL code, use efficient shaders, and minimize unnecessary rendering to ensure a responsive experience.

- **User Interface (UI):** Design user interfaces that are comfortable and easy to interact with in VR and AR environments. Consider the placement of menus, buttons, and other UI elements within the 3D scene.

- **Content Creation:** Create 3D assets and models optimized for web-based VR and AR. Consider the file formats, textures, and level of detail required for a seamless experience.

- **Testing:** Thoroughly test your VR and AR experiences on different devices and browsers to ensure compatibility and performance. Consider factors such as screen resolution, input methods, and tracking capabilities.

Implementing VR and AR in WebGL opens up exciting possibilities for creating interactive and immersive web-based applications. Whether you're building educational simulations, games, or innovative marketing experiences, understanding the principles of WebXR and frameworks like A-Frame can help you deliver compelling and accessible VR and AR content to a broad audience.

Section 14.4: Challenges and Opportunities in VR/AR with WebGL

Implementing Virtual Reality (VR) and Augmented Reality (AR) in WebGL offers exciting possibilities, but it also presents developers with various challenges and opportunities. In this section, we'll explore some of the key obstacles to overcome and the potential benefits to harness when working with VR/AR in WebGL.

Challenges

1. **Performance:** One of the most significant challenges in VR/AR development with WebGL is maintaining high performance. VR and AR experiences require smooth, low-latency rendering to prevent motion sickness and provide an immersive feel. Optimizing shaders, reducing unnecessary rendering, and handling complex 3D models are crucial for achieving good performance.
2. **Cross-Browser Compatibility:** Ensuring that VR/AR experiences work consistently across different web browsers and devices can be challenging. The availability and support of WebXR APIs may vary, and developers need to consider fallback options for users with

incompatible browsers.

3. **User Interface (UI) in 3D Space:** Designing intuitive and comfortable UI elements within the 3D environment of VR/AR is a unique challenge. Developers must consider factors like the placement of menus, buttons, and interaction cues to create a user-friendly experience.
4. **Content Creation:** Creating 3D assets and models optimized for web-based VR/AR can be time-consuming. Developers need to choose suitable file formats, textures, and level-of-detail strategies to balance visual quality with performance.
5. **Interaction Design:** Crafting natural and immersive interactions in VR/AR requires thoughtful design. Designers must consider how users will interact with the environment, whether through controllers, gestures, or voice commands, and ensure that these interactions are intuitive and comfortable.

Opportunities

1. **Accessibility:** WebGL-based VR/AR experiences can be more accessible than native applications because they run directly in web browsers. This accessibility can lead to a broader user base and increased engagement.
2. **Cross-Platform Reach:** Web-based VR/AR experiences can run on various devices, including smartphones, tablets, desktops, and VR headsets. This cross-platform compatibility allows developers to reach a wide audience without the need for platform-specific development.
3. **WebXR Standards:** As WebXR standards continue to evolve, developers can expect improved support and more features for building immersive experiences in web browsers. This ongoing development opens up new

possibilities and enhances the capabilities of web-based VR/AR.

4. **Community and Resources:** The WebGL and WebXR communities offer a wealth of resources, tutorials, and open-source projects. Developers can leverage this collective knowledge to accelerate their VR/AR projects and find solutions to common challenges.
5. **Innovation:** Web-based VR/AR is a space ripe for innovation. Developers have the opportunity to create groundbreaking applications that push the boundaries of what's possible in immersive web experiences. Whether it's education, entertainment, or industry-specific applications, the potential for innovation is vast.

In conclusion, working with VR/AR in WebGL is a dynamic and evolving field that presents both challenges and opportunities. Overcoming performance bottlenecks, ensuring compatibility, and designing engaging user experiences are essential for success. However, the accessibility, cross-platform reach, evolving standards, and potential for innovation make it an exciting domain for developers looking to create immersive web-based content.

Section 14.5: Future Trends in VR/AR Graphics

The field of Virtual Reality (VR) and Augmented Reality (AR) graphics is continually evolving, driven by advancements in hardware, software, and user expectations. In this section, we'll explore some of the exciting future trends and developments in VR/AR graphics.

1. Hardware Advancements

1.1. Improved Haptic Feedback: Future VR/AR hardware is likely to offer more sophisticated haptic feedback, allowing users to feel textures, forces, and interactions more realistically. This will enhance immersion and user engagement.

1.2. Eye-Tracking Technology: Integrated eye-tracking in headsets can enable more natural interactions by determining where users are looking. It can also facilitate foveated rendering, improving rendering efficiency and visual quality.

1.3. Wireless Connectivity: As wireless technologies improve, VR/AR headsets may become completely wireless, providing greater freedom of movement and reducing the setup complexity.

2. Software and Content Creation

2.1. AI-Driven Content Generation: Artificial intelligence (AI) will play a significant role in generating realistic 3D environments and characters. AI can automate content creation, making it easier for developers to create immersive experiences.

2.2. Real-time Ray Tracing: Real-time ray tracing, which simulates the behavior of light in real-time, will become more common in VR/AR graphics. This technology enhances visual realism by accurately modeling lighting, reflections, and shadows.

2.3. User-Generated Content: Platforms for user-generated content creation in VR/AR will grow, allowing users to contribute to and customize their virtual experiences.

3. Interactivity and Social Experiences

3.1. Shared Virtual Worlds: Future VR/AR platforms will focus on creating shared virtual spaces where users can interact with others, attend events, and collaborate in immersive environments.

3.2. Social Presence: Technologies that enhance social presence, such as realistic avatars and natural body language animations, will enable more meaningful and natural social interactions in VR/AR.

4. Applications Across Industries

4.1. Education and Training: VR/AR will see increased adoption in education and training, offering immersive learning experiences, simulations, and skill development across various fields.

4.2. Healthcare: VR/AR applications in healthcare will expand, including surgical training, patient rehabilitation, and telemedicine consultations.

4.3. Architecture and Design: Architects and designers will use VR/AR extensively for designing and visualizing buildings and spaces before construction begins.

5. Ethical Considerations

5.1. Privacy Concerns: As VR/AR becomes more integrated into daily life, privacy concerns related to data collection and surveillance within virtual spaces will need to be addressed.

5.2. Ethical Use: The responsible and ethical use of VR/AR, particularly in areas like education and healthcare, will be a focus to ensure positive outcomes and prevent misuse.

In conclusion, the future of VR/AR graphics is promising, with advancements in hardware, software, and content creation poised to transform how we interact with virtual and augmented environments. These trends will open up new possibilities for applications across industries and lead to more immersive and engaging experiences for users. However, as VR/AR technologies continue to evolve, ethical considerations and responsible development will be essential to ensure that these technologies benefit society as a whole.

Chapter 15: From Desktop to Browser: Porting Strategies

Section 15.1: The Porting Process Explained

Porting graphics applications from a desktop environment to the web browser can be a complex yet rewarding endeavor. This process involves adapting existing code and design to make it compatible with web technologies like WebGL and HTML5. In this section, we'll delve into the intricacies of the porting process and discuss various strategies to ensure a successful transition.

Understanding the Motivation

Before diving into the technical aspects of porting, it's crucial to understand the motivation behind it. Porting allows developers to reach a broader audience by making their applications accessible on the web. This can lead to increased visibility, user engagement, and potentially new revenue streams. Additionally, web-based graphics applications can benefit from the browser's ubiquity, enabling users to access them across different devices and platforms.

Assessing Compatibility

The first step in the porting process is assessing compatibility. Determine whether your existing desktop graphics application can be effectively translated to the web. Some applications may require significant modifications due to differences in architecture and technology stacks. Evaluate the feasibility of porting by considering factors like the complexity of your application, its reliance on platform-specific APIs, and the availability of equivalent web technologies.

Choosing the Right Technology Stack

Selecting the appropriate technology stack is crucial for a successful porting process. WebGL, a JavaScript API for rendering 3D graphics within web browsers, is often the go-to choice for graphics-intensive applications. It provides access to the GPU's capabilities and enables high-performance rendering on the web. Additionally, HTML5 and JavaScript can be used for user interface elements and interactivity.

Refactoring and Code Conversion

Porting typically involves refactoring and code conversion. You may need to rewrite parts of your application's code to make it compatible with web standards. For example, if your desktop application relies on DirectX or OpenGL APIs, you'll need to replace these with WebGL equivalents. This step can be labor-intensive but is necessary for ensuring smooth execution in a web environment.

Addressing Compatibility Issues

During the porting process, you'll likely encounter compatibility issues stemming from differences between desktop and web environments. Common challenges include handling input events, managing resources, and adapting rendering techniques. Addressing these issues requires careful debugging, testing, and optimization to achieve parity with the original application.

Performance Considerations in Porting

Performance is a critical aspect of porting graphics applications to the web. Web-based applications must run smoothly in a variety of browsers and on different hardware configurations. This necessitates optimizing your code, shaders, and assets to ensure efficient execution. Testing on multiple web browsers and devices is essential to identify and resolve performance bottlenecks.

Testing and Deployment Strategies

Once your ported application is ready, thorough testing is essential to ensure a seamless user experience. Testing should encompass various browsers, operating systems, and devices to identify any compatibility or performance issues. Additionally, consider deployment options, such as hosting on web servers or distributing through app stores, to make your application accessible to users.

User Engagement and Feedback

Engaging with users and gathering feedback is crucial after deploying your web-based graphics application. Actively listen to user comments and bug reports, and iterate on your application to address any issues or enhancements. Building a community around your web application can lead to continuous improvements and user satisfaction.

In summary, porting a graphics application from desktop to the web involves careful planning, code adaptation, and thorough testing. By understanding the motivation, choosing the right technology stack, and addressing compatibility and performance considerations, developers can successfully bring their graphics creations to the broader online audience.

Section 15.2: Porting an OpenGL Application to WebGL

Porting an OpenGL application to WebGL is a challenging yet rewarding process that allows you to bring your desktop graphics software to the web. This section will guide you through the steps involved in this transformation, from understanding WebGL to adapting your OpenGL code for web compatibility.

Understanding WebGL

WebGL, short for Web Graphics Library, is a JavaScript API for rendering interactive 2D and 3D graphics within web browsers. It is based on OpenGL ES, a subset of the OpenGL graphics API commonly used in embedded systems and mobile devices. WebGL leverages the GPU's power and is supported by most modern web browsers, making it an excellent choice for porting graphics applications.

Initial Assessment

Before you begin porting, assess your OpenGL application thoroughly. Evaluate its architecture, rendering techniques, and dependencies on platform-specific APIs. Consider the compatibility of your code with WebGL, as there may be differences in how certain features are implemented. Identify areas that need modification or rewriting to work within the web environment.

Code Adaptation

Adapting your OpenGL code for WebGL involves several key steps:

1. **Shader Conversion:** If your OpenGL application uses shaders, you'll need to convert them to GLSL (OpenGL Shading Language) compatible with WebGL. WebGL shaders have some syntactical differences, so be prepared to make adjustments.
2. **Context Creation:** In WebGL, you'll create a rendering context using the canvas element, unlike OpenGL, which typically uses platform-specific windowing systems. This

context is crucial for initializing and managing your WebGL application.

3. **Buffer and Texture Management:** Review how you manage buffers and textures in your OpenGL application and adjust them for WebGL. WebGL has its way of creating and handling these resources.
4. **Rendering Loop:** Adapt your rendering loop to work within the event-driven nature of web applications. In OpenGL, the rendering loop typically runs continuously, while in WebGL, it responds to events like animation frames.

Replacing Platform-Specific APIs

One of the primary challenges in porting OpenGL applications to WebGL is dealing with platform-specific APIs. You'll need to replace these with web-compatible alternatives. For example, if you were using OpenGL's platform-specific input handling, you'll need to switch to web event handling using JavaScript.

Testing and Debugging

Testing is a crucial phase in the porting process. Ensure that your application works correctly across different web browsers, as WebGL support and performance can vary. Use debugging tools available in web browsers to identify and resolve issues. WebGL debugging libraries and frameworks can also be helpful.

Optimization for Web

To ensure good performance in a web environment, consider optimizing your code, shaders, and assets. WebGL applications need to run smoothly on a wide range of devices, so performance tuning is essential. Profiling tools can help identify bottlenecks and areas for improvement.

Web Deployment

Once your OpenGL application is successfully ported to WebGL, consider various deployment options. You can host it on a web server, package it as a Progressive Web App (PWA), or distribute it through app stores. Make your application accessible to a broad audience while ensuring it works seamlessly in different web environments.

User Experience and Feedback

Engage with your users and gather feedback after deploying your WebGL application. Actively address any reported issues or suggestions for improvement. Building a user community around your web application can lead to continuous enhancements and a more satisfying user experience.

In conclusion, porting an OpenGL application to WebGL involves understanding WebGL, assessing your existing code, adapting it for web compatibility, and thorough testing. By replacing platform-specific APIs, optimizing for the web, and actively engaging with users, you can successfully bring your graphics application to the online world.

Section 15.3: Addressing Compatibility Issues

When porting an OpenGL application to WebGL, one of the key challenges is dealing with compatibility issues that arise due to differences in the underlying technologies and APIs. This section will delve into common compatibility issues you may encounter during the porting process and provide strategies for addressing them effectively.

Browser Variability

WebGL support can vary across different web browsers, and each browser may have its own implementation quirks and performance characteristics. To address this issue:

1. **Cross-Browser Testing:** Test your WebGL application on multiple browsers, including Chrome, Firefox, Safari, and Edge. Use browser-specific debugging tools to identify and resolve issues unique to each platform.
2. **Fallback Mechanisms:** Implement fallback mechanisms for browsers that do not support WebGL. This can include displaying a message encouraging users to switch to a WebGL-enabled browser or providing alternative content.
3. **WebGL Feature Detection:** Use feature detection libraries like Modernizr or write custom JavaScript code to check for WebGL support in the user's browser and adjust your application's behavior accordingly.

Security Considerations

WebGL applications run in a sandboxed environment within the browser to prevent security breaches. However, you must still be vigilant about security:

1. **Content Security Policy (CSP):** Implement a CSP in your web application to control which external resources can be loaded and executed. This helps mitigate potential security risks associated with loading external scripts or resources.
2. **Data Validation and Sanitization:** Ensure that user inputs

and data received from external sources are properly validated and sanitized to prevent security vulnerabilities such as cross-site scripting (XSS) attacks.

3. **WebGL Context Security:** WebGL allows shaders to be written in GLSL, which can introduce security risks. Carefully review and validate shaders to prevent potential exploits.

Performance Optimization

WebGL applications need to perform well across various devices and network conditions:

1. **Asset Compression:** Compress textures and other assets to reduce loading times and improve overall performance. Use modern image formats like WebP for better compression.
2. **Minification and Bundling:** Minify JavaScript and CSS files to reduce their size. Consider bundling multiple assets into a single file to minimize network requests.
3. **Texture Atlases:** Use texture atlases to combine multiple textures into a single image, reducing the number of texture swaps and improving rendering efficiency.
4. **LOD (Level of Detail):** Implement level-of-detail techniques to optimize rendering by reducing the complexity of objects when they are distant from the camera.

Input Handling

WebGL applications often require user interaction, and input handling may differ from traditional desktop applications:

1. **Mouse and Touch Events:** Adapt your input handling to

support both mouse and touch events. Ensure that your application responds well to touch gestures on mobile devices.

2. **Keyboard Input:** Implement keyboard event listeners to accommodate keyboard input for interactions that were previously mouse-driven.

File Loading and Asset Management

WebGL applications need to load assets asynchronously, which may require changes in how assets are managed:

1. **Asynchronous Loading:** Use asynchronous techniques to load assets such as textures, models, and shaders to prevent blocking the main thread.
2. **Asset Loading Libraries:** Consider using asset loading libraries or frameworks like glTF for 3D models to simplify asset management and loading.

Debugging and Testing Tools

Take advantage of debugging and testing tools available for web development:

1. **Browser DevTools:** Use browser developer tools to inspect WebGL contexts, debug JavaScript code, and profile application performance.
2. **WebGL Debugging Extensions:** WebGL debugging extensions like WEBGL_debug_renderer_info and WEBGL_debug_shaders can help identify issues in your WebGL code.
3. **Automated Testing:** Implement automated testing using frameworks like Selenium or Puppeteer to ensure your application works as expected across different browsers.

By addressing these compatibility issues and employing best practices for security, performance optimization, input handling, and asset management, you can successfully navigate the challenges of porting your OpenGL application to WebGL while delivering a reliable and engaging web experience to your users.

Section 15.4: Performance Considerations in Porting

When porting an OpenGL application to WebGL, optimizing performance becomes crucial to ensure that your web-based graphics application runs smoothly and efficiently. This section will explore various performance considerations and strategies for addressing them during the porting process.

1. WebGL-Specific Performance Considerations

- **Limited GPU Resources:** WebGL applications share GPU resources with the web page's content and other browser tabs. Be mindful of GPU memory and processing limitations when designing your application.

- **Texture Size Constraints:** WebGL may have constraints on texture sizes, depending on the user's hardware and browser. Ensure that your textures are within acceptable size limits.

2. Shader Performance

- **Simplify Shaders:** WebGL shaders must be more streamlined than their OpenGL counterparts. Simplify and optimize shaders to reduce computation and memory usage.

- **Avoid Conditional Branching:** Excessive conditional branching in shaders can hinder performance. Minimize branching and use shader constants for optimization.

- **Precision Control:** WebGL shaders may have different precision constraints compared to OpenGL. Explicitly specify precision qualifiers to optimize performance while maintaining visual quality.

3. Geometry and Vertex Processing

- **Reduce Vertex Count:** Reduce the number of vertices in your 3D models, especially for objects that are far from the camera. Implement Level of Detail (LOD) techniques to dynamically simplify geometry.

- **Instancing:** Utilize WebGL's instancing capabilities to efficiently render multiple instances of the same object with a single draw call.

4. Texture and Asset Optimization

- **Texture Compression:** Use texture compression formats (e.g., ETC2, PVRTC) to reduce texture memory usage and improve loading times.

- **Mipmap Generation:** Generate mipmaps for textures to enhance texture sampling performance, especially for objects at varying distances from the camera.

5. Rendering Techniques

- **Batch Rendering:** Implement batch rendering to minimize state changes and reduce draw calls. Group objects with similar shaders and textures to optimize rendering performance.

- **Offscreen Rendering:** Be cautious with offscreen rendering as it can be costly in WebGL. Minimize its usage or implement techniques like framebuffer pooling for efficiency.

6. Asynchronous Loading

- **Resource Loading:** Load assets asynchronously to prevent blocking the main thread. Implement loading screens or progress indicators to improve the user experience during asset loading.

- **Lazy Loading:** Load assets on-demand, especially for large or non-essential resources, to reduce initial load times.

7. JavaScript Performance

- **Minification and Compression:** Minify and compress JavaScript files to reduce file sizes and improve parsing and execution times.

- **Memory Management:** Optimize memory usage by avoiding memory leaks and efficiently managing data structures.

8. Testing and Profiling

- **Browser DevTools:** Use browser developer tools to profile and analyze your application's performance. Identify bottlenecks and areas for improvement.

- **Performance Profiling:** Implement performance profiling tools within your application to monitor frame rates, memory usage, and other critical metrics.

- **Benchmarking:** Regularly benchmark your WebGL application on different devices and browsers to ensure consistent and satisfactory performance.

9. User Experience

- **Responsive Design:** Ensure that your WebGL application provides a responsive user experience across various screen sizes and orientations.

- **Frame Rate Targeting:** Adjust your application to target a reasonable and consistent frame rate to prevent stuttering or jarring experiences.

By carefully considering and addressing these performance considerations during the porting process, you can optimize your WebGL application's performance, delivering a seamless and engaging experience to users across a wide range of devices and browsers. Performance optimization is an ongoing process, so continue to monitor and fine-tune your application as needed to maintain optimal performance.

Section 15.5: Testing and Deployment Strategies

After porting your OpenGL application to WebGL, it's essential to plan your testing and deployment strategies to ensure that your web-based graphics application reaches your target audience smoothly and without issues. This section explores various strategies and best practices for testing and deploying WebGL applications effectively.

1. Cross-Browser and Cross-Device Testing

- **Browser Compatibility:** Test your WebGL application on multiple web browsers, including Chrome, Firefox, Safari, Edge, and others. Each browser may have slightly different WebGL implementations, so ensure consistent functionality.

- **Device Testing:** Verify that your application works well on various devices, including desktops, laptops, tablets, and mobile phones. Consider different screen sizes, resolutions, and touch interactions.

2. Responsive Design Testing

- **Viewport Flexibility:** Check how your application adapts to different viewport sizes. Ensure that it remains visually appealing and functional across various screen dimensions.

- **Orientation Handling:** Test your WebGL application's behavior when the user switches between portrait and landscape orientations on mobile devices.

3. Performance Benchmarking

- **Frame Rate Analysis:** Use performance monitoring tools to analyze and benchmark the frame rate, memory usage, and CPU utilization of your application under different conditions and on various devices.

- **Load Testing:** Simulate high loads by deploying your application to multiple users simultaneously to identify potential bottlenecks and server capacity issues.

4. User Experience Testing

- **Usability Testing:** Conduct usability testing with real users to gather feedback on the user interface, controls, and overall user experience. Make necessary adjustments based on user input.

- **Accessibility Testing:** Ensure that your WebGL application complies with accessibility standards, making it usable for individuals with disabilities. Test with screen readers and other assistive technologies.

5. Security and Privacy Testing

- **Security Auditing:** Perform security audits and penetration testing to identify and address potential vulnerabilities in your WebGL application.

- **Privacy Compliance:** Ensure that your application respects user privacy and complies with data protection regulations. Implement data anonymization and encryption where necessary.

6. Deployment Strategies

- **Content Delivery Networks (CDNs):** Utilize CDNs to distribute your WebGL application's assets and improve load times by serving content from geographically distributed servers.

• **Version Control:** Use version control systems like Git to manage your project's source code and collaborate with team members effectively.

• **Continuous Integration/Continuous Deployment (CI/CD):** Set up CI/CD pipelines to automate testing and deployment processes, ensuring a smooth workflow for updates and improvements.

• **Progressive Web App (PWA):** Consider turning your WebGL application into a PWA, enabling offline access, improved performance, and app-like experiences on supported platforms.

7. Documentation and User Support

• **User Guides:** Create comprehensive user guides and documentation for your WebGL application, including installation instructions, troubleshooting tips, and FAQs.

• **User Support Channels:** Establish communication channels, such as email support or forums, to assist users with inquiries and issues they may encounter while using your application.

8. Performance Monitoring

• **Real-Time Monitoring:** Implement real-time performance monitoring tools that allow you to track your application's performance, detect errors, and respond promptly to issues.

• **Error Reporting:** Set up error reporting systems to receive notifications about errors and exceptions in your

WebGL application. Use this data to diagnose and fix issues.

9. User Feedback and Iteration

- **Feedback Loops:** Encourage users to provide feedback on your application. Use this feedback to make iterative improvements and address any issues that arise.

- **Regular Updates:** Continuously update your WebGL application to fix bugs, enhance performance, and introduce new features based on user feedback and emerging technologies.

By implementing these testing and deployment strategies, you can ensure that your WebGL application delivers a positive and reliable experience to users while maintaining its performance and security standards. Regularly monitor and iterate on your application to keep it up to date and aligned with evolving web standards and user expectations.

Chapter 16: Security and Privacy in WebGL

Section 16.1: Understanding Security in Web-Based Graphics

Security and privacy are paramount considerations when developing web-based graphics applications using WebGL. WebGL applications run within web browsers and have access to various resources, making them susceptible to potential security threats and privacy concerns. This section delves into the fundamentals of security in web-based graphics, highlighting common security concerns and best practices for mitigating risks.

Understanding Security in Web-Based Graphics

WebGL applications are subject to the security model of web browsers, which is designed to protect users from malicious code and unauthorized access to their devices and data. Key aspects of security in web-based graphics include:

1. **Same-Origin Policy (SOP):** Browsers enforce the SOP, which restricts web pages from making requests to domains different from the one that served the web page. WebGL adheres to this policy, ensuring that graphics applications cannot access resources from other origins without proper permissions.
2. **Cross-Site Scripting (XSS) Attacks:** WebGL applications can be vulnerable to XSS attacks if they don't properly validate and sanitize user-generated input. Attackers may inject malicious scripts into the application, compromising user data and security.
3. **Content Security Policy (CSP):** CSP is a security feature that helps prevent XSS attacks by specifying which sources of content are considered trusted. Implementing CSP headers can enhance the security of WebGL applications.
4. **WebGL Security Contexts:** WebGL provides security contexts to isolate different applications and prevent them from accessing each other's data. Developers should be aware of these contexts and how to manage them effectively.
5. **WebGL Extensions:** Some WebGL extensions may have security implications. Developers should carefully evaluate the use of extensions and ensure they do not introduce vulnerabilities.
6. **Browser Updates:** Regularly update the web browser used

to run WebGL applications to benefit from security patches and updates. Outdated browsers may expose users to known vulnerabilities.

7. **Data Transmission:** When transmitting data between the client and server, use secure protocols like HTTPS to encrypt data in transit. This prevents eavesdropping and data interception.
8. **Privacy Concerns:** WebGL applications should respect user privacy by not collecting sensitive information without consent. Clearly communicate privacy practices and obtain user consent when necessary.
9. **Resource Loading:** Be cautious when loading external resources like textures or models. Ensure that the sources are trusted and do not pose security risks.
10. **Code Review:** Conduct thorough code reviews to identify and address potential security vulnerabilities in your WebGL application's source code.
11. **Third-Party Libraries:** Be mindful of third-party libraries and dependencies, as they can introduce security risks. Keep them up to date and review their security track record.

By understanding these security considerations and following best practices, developers can create WebGL applications that provide a safe and secure user experience. Security should be an ongoing concern, and developers should stay informed about emerging threats and vulnerabilities in web-based graphics technology.

Section 16.2: Common Security Concerns in WebGL

WebGL, while a powerful and versatile technology for web-based graphics, presents several common security concerns that developers must be aware of and address to ensure the safety of their applications and users. In this section, we will explore these security concerns and discuss strategies for mitigating them.

1. Cross-Origin Resource Sharing (CORS) Issues

One of the fundamental security measures in web-based graphics is the Same-Origin Policy (SOP), which restricts resources from being loaded from domains other than the one serving the web page. WebGL applications may need to load textures, models, or other resources from different domains, potentially leading to CORS issues. Developers should set up proper CORS headers on the server to allow or deny resource loading from specific origins, ensuring that only trusted sources are accessed.

```
// Example CORS configuration in Express.js middleware

const express = require('express');

const app = express();

// Allow resource loading from specific origins

app.use((req, res, next) => {

res.header('Access-Control-Allow-Origin', 'https://trusted-domain.com');

res.header('Access-Control-Allow-Methods', 'GET');
```

```
next();
});
// ...
```

2. Injection Attacks

WebGL applications that accept user input, such as shader code or filenames for resource loading, are susceptible to injection attacks like Cross-Site Scripting (XSS). Developers must validate and sanitize user input thoroughly to prevent malicious code injection.

```
// Example of input validation and sanitization
function validateInput(input) {
// Check for potentially harmful content
if (/[\&\<\>\"\'\`]/.test(input)) {
throw new Error('Invalid input');
}
return input;
}
```

3. WebGL Debugging and Development Extensions

While WebGL debugging and development extensions can be useful during development, they can pose security risks if left enabled in production. These extensions may expose sensitive information or provide attackers with tools for profiling and exploiting vulnerabilities. Ensure that debugging and development extensions are disabled in the production environment.

```
// Disable WebGL debugging and development extensions

const canvas = document.getElementById('webgl-canvas');

const gl = canvas.getContext('webgl', { debug: false, preserveDrawingBuffer: false });
```

4. Secure Data Transmission

When transmitting data between the client and server in WebGL applications, it's essential to use secure protocols like HTTPS to encrypt data in transit. Unencrypted communication may expose sensitive user data to eavesdropping and interception.

```
<!—Enforce HTTPS for WebGL application—>

<meta http-equiv="Content-Security-Policy" content="upgrade-insecure-requests">
```

5. Proper Error Handling

Effective error handling is crucial for security. Avoid exposing detailed error messages to users, as they can reveal implementation details and potentially assist attackers. Instead, implement graceful error handling and log errors securely on the server.

```
// Avoid exposing detailed error messages

app.use((err, req, res, next) => {

console.error(err.stack);

res.status(500).send('Something went wrong!');
```

```
});
```

By addressing these common security concerns and following best practices, developers can enhance the security of their WebGL applications and protect users from potential threats. Security should be an integral part of the development process, and ongoing vigilance is essential to stay ahead of emerging security challenges.

Section 16.3: Implementing Secure WebGL Applications

Developing secure WebGL applications requires a comprehensive approach to mitigate potential security risks. In this section, we will explore best practices and techniques for implementing secure WebGL applications.

1. Enforce HTTPS

One of the fundamental steps in ensuring the security of WebGL applications is to host them on servers that support HTTPS (HTTP Secure). HTTPS encrypts data transmitted between the client and the server, protecting against eavesdropping and data interception. Many browsers require HTTPS for certain WebGL features to work correctly, and using HTTPS is considered a best practice for all web applications.

To enable HTTPS, you'll need to obtain an SSL/TLS certificate for your domain and configure your web server to use it. Popular web server software like Apache and Nginx provide documentation on setting up HTTPS.

2. Sanitize User Input

WebGL applications that accept user input, such as text fields or filenames, should implement thorough input validation and sanitization. Input validation ensures that the data conforms to expected formats, while sanitization removes or escapes potentially harmful characters to prevent injection attacks like Cross-Site Scripting (XSS).

```
// Example of input validation and sanitization in JavaScript

function sanitizeInput(input) {

// Remove potentially harmful characters

return input.replace(/<script>|<\/script>/gi, '');

}

const userInput = '<script>alert("XSS attack");</script>';

const sanitizedInput = sanitizeInput(userInput);
```

3. Content Security Policy (CSP)

Implementing a Content Security Policy (CSP) is an effective way to mitigate various security risks in WebGL applications. CSP allows you to specify which sources of content are trusted and which are not. It helps prevent XSS attacks by restricting the sources from which scripts can be executed and resources can be loaded.

```
<!—Example of a Content Security Policy header—>

<meta http-equiv="Content-Security-Policy" content="default-src 'self' trusted-domain.com; script-src 'self' trusted-scripts.com; img-src 'self' data:">
```

4. Disable WebGL Debugging Extensions

While WebGL debugging extensions are valuable during development, they can expose sensitive information and potentially assist attackers. To enhance security in production, make sure to disable WebGL debugging extensions. You can do this by creating the WebGL context with specific attributes.

```
// Disable WebGL debugging extensions

const canvas = document.getElementById('webgl-canvas');

const gl = canvas.getContext('webgl', { debug: false,
preserveDrawingBuffer: false });
```

5. Limit Permissions

Limiting the permissions granted to WebGL applications is crucial for security. Avoid using overly permissive CORS headers and grant access only to trusted origins when loading resources. Additionally, restrict the capabilities of shaders to prevent them from consuming excessive resources or causing performance issues.

By following these best practices and implementing security measures, developers can create WebGL applications that are resilient against common security threats. WebGL's power and versatility can be harnessed safely when combined with a robust security strategy. Keep security in mind throughout the development lifecycle to protect your users and data.

Section 16.4: Privacy Considerations in Graphics Programming

Privacy is a growing concern in the world of web-based graphics programming. As WebGL and OpenGL applications become more sophisticated and data-driven, it's essential to address privacy considerations. In this section, we'll explore various aspects of privacy in graphics programming and discuss strategies to protect user data.

1. User Data Collection

Graphics applications often interact with user data, including user-generated content, input, and preferences. It's crucial to be transparent about what data your application collects and how it is used. Clearly communicate your data collection and privacy policies to users through your application's terms of service or privacy policy.

2. Geolocation and User Tracking

Some graphics applications, especially those integrated with mapping or location-based services, may request access to a user's geolocation. Always request user consent before accessing sensitive location data. Additionally, avoid unnecessary tracking of user behavior, as excessive tracking can raise privacy concerns. If tracking is essential, anonymize data and offer users opt-out options.

3. Cookies and Local Storage

Web-based graphics applications often use cookies and local storage to store user preferences and session data. Be mindful of the data you store in cookies and local storage, as it can potentially be accessed by other scripts or third parties. Follow best practices for securing cookies and local storage and consider using HTTP-only and secure cookies when appropriate.

```
// Example of setting an HTTP-only and secure cookie in JavaScript

document.cookie = "sessionToken=xyz; path=/; HttpOnly; Secure";
```

4. Third-Party Integrations

Graphics applications sometimes integrate third-party services or APIs for various functionalities. When doing so, review the privacy policies and data handling practices of these third parties. Ensure that they align with your application's privacy standards and communicate to users which third-party services are being used.

5. Data Encryption

When transmitting sensitive data between the client and server, use encryption mechanisms like SSL/TLS to protect data in transit. This prevents eavesdropping and man-in-the-middle attacks that can compromise user privacy.

6. User Consent and Permissions

Respect user consent and permissions for accessing device features, such as the camera, microphone, or file system. Only request permissions when necessary and clearly explain why they are needed. Always provide users with the option to revoke these permissions.

7. Data Retention and Deletion

Define clear policies regarding data retention and deletion. Avoid retaining user data indefinitely, and regularly review and delete data that is no longer needed. Allow users to request the deletion of their data and provide mechanisms for them to do so.

8. Compliance with Regulations

Stay informed about privacy regulations that may apply to your graphics application, such as the General Data Protection Regulation (GDPR) in Europe or the California Consumer Privacy Act (CCPA) in the United States. Ensure compliance with relevant privacy laws and provide users with the necessary rights and controls over their data.

By addressing privacy considerations in graphics programming, developers can build trust with users and protect sensitive information. Privacy-conscious design and transparent communication about data handling practices are essential for creating applications that respect user privacy and comply with privacy regulations.

Section 16.5: Best Practices for Secure and Private Graphics

As we conclude our discussion on security and privacy in graphics programming, it's important to summarize some best practices that can help you ensure the security and privacy of your graphics applications. These practices are essential for building trust with users, complying with regulations, and maintaining the integrity of your applications.

1. Regularly Update Dependencies

Keep your graphics libraries, frameworks, and third-party dependencies up to date. Vulnerabilities can emerge over time, and updates often include security patches. Regularly monitoring for updates and promptly applying them can mitigate security risks.

2. Implement Authentication and Authorization

If your graphics application involves user accounts or access control, implement robust authentication and authorization mechanisms. Use secure password hashing, enforce strong password policies, and implement role-based access control to ensure that users only have access to the data and features they are authorized to use.

3. Input Validation and Sanitization

Always validate and sanitize user inputs to prevent injection attacks such as SQL injection or cross-site scripting (XSS). Use libraries and frameworks that offer built-in input validation functions to minimize the risk of vulnerabilities.

4. Secure File Uploads

If your application allows file uploads, validate and restrict the types of files that can be uploaded. Store uploaded files in a secure location outside of the web root directory to prevent unauthorized access. Implement proper file handling and consider using content security headers to mitigate risks associated with content types.

```
// Example of restricting file types in PHP

$allowedTypes = ['image/jpeg', 'image/png', 'application/pdf'];
```

```
if (in_array($_FILES['uploadedFile']['type'], $allowedTypes)) {
// Process the uploaded file
} else {
// Reject the file
}
```

5. Use Security Headers

Implement security headers in your web server or application to provide an extra layer of protection. Common security headers include Content Security Policy (CSP), X-Content-Type-Options, and X-Frame-Options. These headers can help prevent various types of attacks, including XSS and clickjacking.

6. Monitor and Audit

Regularly monitor your graphics application for suspicious activities or security incidents. Implement logging and auditing mechanisms to track user actions and system events. These logs can be valuable for investigating security breaches and identifying vulnerabilities.

7. Educate Your Team

Ensure that your development team is educated about security best practices. Conduct security training and promote a culture of security awareness within your organization. Encourage developers to stay informed about the latest security threats and mitigation techniques.

8. Penetration Testing

Consider conducting regular penetration testing or security assessments of your graphics applications. Engage with security experts to identify vulnerabilities and weaknesses that may not be apparent through regular code reviews.

9. Incident Response Plan

Develop an incident response plan that outlines how your team will respond to security incidents or breaches. Having a well-defined plan can help minimize damage and reduce downtime in the event of an attack.

10. Privacy by Design

Integrate privacy considerations into the design and development of your graphics applications from the beginning. Conduct privacy impact assessments and ensure that data protection measures are built into the core of your application.

By following these best practices, you can create graphics applications that are not only visually impressive but also secure and respectful of user privacy. Remember that security and privacy are ongoing processes, and it's important to stay vigilant and adaptable in the face of evolving threats and regulations.

Section 17.1: Building Scalable Graphics Applications

Scalability is a critical consideration when developing graphics applications, especially if you anticipate growth in users, data, or features over time. Building scalable graphics applications ensures that your software can handle increased demands without sacrificing performance or user experience. In this section, we'll explore the key principles and strategies for building scalable graphics applications.

Understanding Scalability

Scalability refers to the ability of an application to handle increasing workloads while maintaining acceptable performance levels. Graphics applications, whether they are desktop-based or web-based, often face scalability challenges due to factors like larger datasets, higher user loads, and evolving requirements.

Design for Modularity

Modularity is a fundamental principle of scalability. Break your graphics application into smaller, independent modules or components. Each module should have a well-defined purpose and interface. This allows you to scale individual components independently, making it easier to add new features or optimize existing ones.

Load Balancing

In web-based graphics applications, distributing user requests and traffic across multiple servers or instances can significantly improve scalability. Load balancers help ensure that no single server is overwhelmed with requests, leading to better performance and fault tolerance.

Caching and Content Delivery Networks (CDNs)

Implement caching mechanisms to store frequently accessed data or graphics assets. Caching reduces the load on your server and accelerates content delivery. Consider using CDNs to distribute static assets like images and scripts geographically, reducing latency for users worldwide.

Database Scaling

If your graphics application relies on a database, choose a scalable database system or implement database scaling techniques. Options like database sharding, replication, and NoSQL databases can help handle larger datasets and increased query loads.

Asynchronous Processing

Use asynchronous processing for time-consuming tasks that don't need to block the main application thread. This can include image processing, file uploads, or background rendering. Asynchronous operations prevent your application from becoming unresponsive under heavy loads.

```
# Python example using asyncio for asynchronous tasks

import asyncio

async def process_image(image_data):

# Perform image processing asynchronously

await asyncio.sleep(5)

return processed_image_data
```

```
# Start the asynchronous task

asyncio.create_task(process_image(image_data))
```

Horizontal and Vertical Scaling

Horizontal scaling involves adding more servers or instances to your infrastructure to distribute the load. Vertical scaling means upgrading the existing server or instance to handle more resources. The choice between these two approaches depends on your application's specific requirements.

Monitoring and Auto-Scaling

Implement monitoring solutions to track the performance and resource utilization of your graphics application. Use auto-scaling mechanisms to dynamically adjust resources based on traffic and workload. Cloud providers offer auto-scaling services that can automatically add or remove instances as needed.

Testing for Scalability

Regularly test your graphics application's scalability using load testing tools and scenarios that simulate real-world usage patterns. Identify bottlenecks and performance limitations, and use the results to fine-tune your scalability strategies.

Documentation and Knowledge Sharing

Document your application's scalability architecture, best practices, and lessons learned. Share this knowledge with your development team and stakeholders to ensure that scalability remains a priority as your application evolves.

Scalability is not a one-time effort but an ongoing consideration throughout the lifecycle of your graphics application. By following these principles and strategies, you can build graphics applications that can grow and adapt to meet the demands of your users and changing requirements.

Section 17.2: Maintaining and Updating OpenGL Projects

Maintaining and updating OpenGL projects is a crucial aspect of long-term graphics application development. As technology evolves and user requirements change, your OpenGL projects may need continuous improvements, bug fixes, and updates to stay relevant and efficient. In this section, we'll explore key strategies and best practices for maintaining and updating OpenGL projects effectively.

Version Compatibility

OpenGL evolves over time, with each version introducing new features and enhancements. It's essential to consider version compatibility when maintaining your OpenGL projects. If you're working on an older project, you may need to update it to use newer OpenGL versions to take advantage of performance improvements and new capabilities. However, be mindful of potential incompatibilities and deprecated features when upgrading.

Dependency Management

OpenGL projects often rely on various libraries and dependencies, such as graphics drivers and third-party libraries like GLFW or

GLEW. Ensure that you keep these dependencies up to date to benefit from bug fixes, security patches, and performance enhancements. Utilize dependency management tools like CMake, Conan, or package managers specific to your development environment to streamline this process.

Code Refactoring

Over time, your OpenGL project's codebase may become complex and challenging to maintain. Regularly review and refactor your code to improve readability, maintainability, and performance. Identify and eliminate code smells, duplicate code, and unnecessary abstractions. Break down monolithic functions into smaller, reusable components for better code organization.

Testing and Quality Assurance

Implement robust testing and quality assurance processes to catch and fix issues promptly. Use unit tests, integration tests, and automated testing frameworks to ensure that code changes do not introduce new bugs. Consider implementing continuous integration (CI) pipelines to automatically build and test your OpenGL project with each code commit.

```
// Example using the Catch2 C++ testing framework

TEST_CASE("OpenGL project rendering test", "[rendering]") {

// Initialize OpenGL context and resources

// Render a scene

// Verify the expected output
```

```
REQUIRE(renderedFrameIsValid());
}
```

Documentation and Comments

Maintain comprehensive documentation for your OpenGL project. Document code functions, classes, and libraries, and provide usage examples. Proper documentation helps new team members understand the project and accelerates the debugging and development process.

Version Control

Use version control systems like Git to track changes and collaborate with other developers efficiently. Create branches for new features, bug fixes, or experiments to isolate changes before merging them into the main codebase. Follow version control best practices, such as writing descriptive commit messages and keeping the commit history clean.

Performance Optimization

Regularly profile and optimize your OpenGL project for better performance. Identify bottlenecks using profiling tools and address them by optimizing critical code paths. Consider using performance analysis tools like NVIDIA Nsight or AMD Radeon GPU Profiler to gain insights into GPU performance.

Security Updates

Stay vigilant about security vulnerabilities related to OpenGL and its dependencies. Monitor security advisories and apply security updates promptly to protect your OpenGL project from potential threats. Security should be a top priority, especially if your project handles sensitive data.

Long-Term Planning

Create a roadmap for the long-term development of your OpenGL project. Define clear objectives, prioritize features and improvements, and allocate resources effectively. Plan for backward compatibility to ensure that future updates do not break existing functionality.

User Feedback

Engage with your project's user community and gather feedback. User feedback can help you identify issues and prioritize enhancements based on actual user needs. Maintain open channels of communication to address user concerns promptly.

Maintaining and updating OpenGL projects is an ongoing process that requires diligence and a proactive approach. By following these best practices, you can ensure that your graphics application remains stable, efficient, and capable of meeting evolving requirements and user expectations.

Section 17.3: Maintaining and Updating WebGL Projects

Maintaining and updating WebGL projects is essential to keep web-based graphics applications running smoothly and securely. In this section, we'll explore key strategies and best practices for effectively maintaining and updating your WebGL projects.

Version Compatibility

WebGL evolves over time, with each new version introducing enhancements and improvements. When maintaining WebGL projects, it's crucial to consider version compatibility. Older projects may need updates to use newer versions of WebGL to take advantage of performance optimizations and new features. However, be cautious of potential incompatibilities and deprecated functions when upgrading.

Dependency Management

WebGL projects often rely on various web technologies, such as HTML, CSS, and JavaScript libraries. Ensure that you keep these dependencies up to date to benefit from bug fixes, security patches, and performance enhancements. Use dependency management tools like npm or yarn to streamline the process of updating JavaScript libraries.

Code Refactoring

Over time, the codebase of your WebGL project may become complex and challenging to maintain. Regularly review and refactor your code to enhance readability, maintainability, and performance. Identify and eliminate code duplication, reduce complexity, and improve the organization of your code.

Testing and Quality Assurance

Implement rigorous testing and quality assurance processes to detect and rectify issues promptly. Use unit tests, integration tests, and end-to-end tests to ensure that code changes do not introduce new bugs. Continuous integration (CI) pipelines can automate building and testing your WebGL project with each code commit.

```
// Example using Jest for JavaScript testing

test('WebGL project rendering test', () => {

// Initialize WebGL context and resources

// Render a scene

// Verify the expected output

expect(renderedFrameIsValid()).toBe(true);

});
```

Documentation and Comments

Maintain comprehensive documentation for your WebGL project. Document JavaScript functions, classes, and libraries, and provide usage examples. Well-documented code helps both your team and external contributors understand the project and facilitates debugging and development.

Version Control

Use version control systems like Git to manage changes and collaborate with other developers effectively. Create branches for new features, bug fixes, or experiments to isolate changes before merging them into the main codebase. Follow version control best practices, such as writing clear commit messages and keeping the commit history organized.

Performance Optimization

Regularly profile and optimize your WebGL project for improved performance. Identify performance bottlenecks using profiling tools and optimize critical code paths. Utilize browser developer tools to analyze and optimize JavaScript execution and GPU rendering performance.

Security Updates

Stay vigilant about security vulnerabilities related to WebGL and its dependencies. Keep an eye on security advisories and apply security updates promptly to safeguard your WebGL project against potential threats. Security should be a top priority, especially if your project handles user data or sensitive information.

Long-Term Planning

Create a long-term development plan for your WebGL project. Define clear objectives, prioritize features and improvements, and allocate resources effectively. Consider backward compatibility to ensure that future updates do not break existing functionality and user experiences.

User Feedback

Engage with your project's user community and gather feedback. User feedback can help you identify issues and prioritize enhancements based on actual user needs. Maintain open channels of communication to address user concerns promptly.

Maintaining and updating WebGL projects is an ongoing process that requires proactive efforts to ensure that web-based graphics applications remain stable, performant, and secure. By following these best practices, you can navigate the challenges of maintaining web graphics projects effectively.

Section 17.4: Version Control and Collaboration in Graphics Projects

Version control and collaboration are essential aspects of maintaining and developing graphics projects, including those involving WebGL. In this section, we'll explore the significance of version control systems and collaborative workflows for managing and enhancing WebGL applications.

Version Control Systems

Version control systems (VCS), such as Git, are fundamental tools for tracking changes, managing project history, and collaborating with a team. They provide a structured way to store different versions of your project's source code and assets.

Benefits of Using Version Control:

- **Change Tracking:** VCS allows you to track changes made to your WebGL project over time. Each change is documented, making it easier to understand who did what and when.

- **Branching and Merging:** VCS enables developers to work on separate branches of the project simultaneously. Branches can be used for new features, bug fixes, or experiments. Merging branches back into the main codebase ensures that changes are integrated smoothly.

- **Code Revert:** If an issue arises, you can easily revert to a previous version of your project to restore functionality. This is invaluable for troubleshooting and addressing unexpected problems.

- **Collaboration:** VCS facilitates collaboration among team members, whether they are working in the same location or remotely. Multiple developers can work on different aspects of the project without interfering with each other.

Git as a Version Control System

Git is one of the most widely used version control systems and is well-suited for graphics projects. It offers a distributed architecture, meaning that every developer has a complete copy of the project's history on their local machine. Here are some Git concepts:

- **Repository (Repo):** A Git repository is where your project is stored, including all its history, files, and directories. There are local repositories (on your computer) and remote repositories (on a server, e.g., GitHub or GitLab).

- **Commit:** A commit is a snapshot of your project at a specific point in time. Each commit has a unique identifier (SHA-1 hash) and includes changes made to the project.

- **Branch:** A branch is a separate line of development in Git. You can create branches for new features or bug fixes.

The main branch, often called master or main, represents the stable version of your project.

• **Pull Request (PR):** In collaborative environments like GitHub, a pull request is a request to merge changes from one branch into another. It allows for code review and discussion before merging.

Collaborative Workflows

Collaboration in graphics projects often involves designers, developers, and other stakeholders. Here's a simplified collaborative workflow:

1. **Create a Repository:** Start by creating a Git repository for your WebGL project. This can be hosted on platforms like GitHub, GitLab, or Bitbucket.
2. **Branching:** Developers create branches for specific tasks or features. For example, a developer might create a branch called feature-new-effects to work on adding new visual effects to the project.
3. **Development:** Developers work on their respective branches, making changes and committing them. Regular commits help in maintaining a detailed history of changes.
4. **Code Review:** Once a task is complete, the developer opens a pull request (PR) for code review. Other team members can review the changes and provide feedback.
5. **Merging:** After the code review process, the changes are merged into the main branch (master or main). It's important to resolve any conflicts that may arise during merging.
6. **Deployment:** When a significant set of changes is merged into the main branch, you can trigger automated

deployment processes to update the WebGL application on a web server.

By using version control and collaborative workflows effectively, teams can streamline development, ensure code quality, and maintain a well-organized history of changes for their WebGL projects. This approach helps manage complexity and fosters collaboration among team members.

Section 17.5: Long-Term Strategies for Scalable Development

Long-term strategies for scalable development are crucial for the success and sustainability of WebGL projects. As WebGL applications evolve and grow in complexity, developers and teams need to adopt practices and approaches that ensure scalability, maintainability, and future-proofing. In this section, we'll discuss key strategies for managing long-term WebGL projects.

1. Modular Architecture

One of the fundamental principles of scalable development is a modular architecture. Break your WebGL project into smaller, reusable modules or components. Each module should have a specific responsibility, making it easier to understand, test, and maintain. This modular approach allows for better code organization and promotes code reuse.

```
// Example of a modular WebGL component

class WebGLRenderer {

constructor() {
```

// Initialize WebGL context, shaders, and buffers

}

render() {

// Render the scene

}

// Other methods for setting up and managing WebGL

}

2. Documentation

Maintaining comprehensive documentation is essential for long-term project success. Document your code, API, and project structure. Include comments, explanations, and usage examples. A well-documented project is more accessible to new team members and ensures that knowledge is not lost over time.

```javascript
/**
* Calculate the normal vector of a triangle given its vertices.
* @param {vec3} v0 - Vertex 0
* @param {vec3} v1 - Vertex 1
* @param {vec3} v2 - Vertex 2
* @returns {vec3} - Normal vector of the triangle
*/
function calculateNormal(v0, v1, v2) {
```

```
// Calculate and return the normal vector

}
```

3. **Testing and Continuous Integration (CI)**

Implement a robust testing strategy and set up a CI pipeline for your WebGL project. Automated tests ensure that new changes don't introduce regressions or bugs. CI tools can run tests automatically whenever changes are pushed to the repository, providing early feedback on the project's health.

4. **Version Control and Collaboration (Revisited)**

Continuing from Section 17.4, version control and collaboration remain critical in the long term. Regularly update dependencies, apply security patches, and keep the project aligned with evolving web standards. Collaboration ensures that multiple team members can contribute to maintenance and improvements.

5. **Performance Monitoring and Optimization**

As WebGL projects expand, performance optimization becomes an ongoing task. Implement performance monitoring tools to identify bottlenecks and areas for improvement. Regularly profile your application to optimize critical code paths, reduce memory usage, and enhance rendering performance.

6. **Compatibility and Browser Support**

Maintain compatibility with modern web browsers and devices. Regularly test your WebGL application on different browsers and platforms to ensure a consistent user experience. Consider using feature detection and graceful degradation to handle older browsers gracefully.

```javascript
// Example of feature detection for WebGL support
if (window.WebGLRenderingContext) {
// WebGL is supported, initialize your WebGL application
} else {
// WebGL is not supported, provide a fallback or alternative content
}
```

7. Community Engagement

Engage with the WebGL and graphics programming communities. Stay updated on emerging technologies, best practices, and industry trends. Participate in discussions, forums, and conferences to gain insights and share knowledge.

8. Security and Privacy

Continuously monitor and address security and privacy concerns. Regularly review your codebase for vulnerabilities, apply security patches, and follow best practices to protect user data and maintain user trust.

9. Backup and Disaster Recovery

Implement backup and disaster recovery strategies to safeguard your WebGL project's data and assets. Regularly back up your source code, assets, and databases to prevent data loss in case of unforeseen events.

By following these long-term strategies, you can ensure that your WebGL project remains robust, scalable, and adaptable to future changes and challenges. Scalable development practices help you meet evolving user expectations and maintain the quality and performance of your WebGL applications over time.

Chapter 18: Community and Open Source Contributions

Section 18.1: The Role of Community in Graphics Development

In the world of graphics programming, the community plays a vital role in shaping the landscape, sharing knowledge, and fostering innovation. This section delves into the significance of the community in graphics development and explores how it contributes to the growth and improvement of OpenGL and WebGL.

1. Sharing Knowledge and Expertise

One of the primary functions of the graphics development community is knowledge sharing. Developers, enthusiasts, and experts regularly exchange information, best practices, and solutions to common challenges. Online forums, blogs, and social media platforms serve as hubs for discussions, Q&A sessions, and tutorials.

''' *javascript*

// Example of a community forum discussion

User1: "I'm having trouble with WebGL shaders. Can someone help?"

User2: "Sure! Can you share your shader code? I'll take a look."

2. Open Source Collaboration

Open source projects are at the heart **of** the graphics community. Many graphics libraries and tools, such **as** Three.js, Babylon.js, and

GLFW, are open source and benefit **from** contributions **from** developers worldwide. Community members contribute code, report issues, and collaborate on enhancements.

```markdown

```javascript

*// Example of an open source contribution*

*// Developer submits a pull request to fix a bug in an open source WebGL library*

### **3. Building Resources and Documentation**

The community actively participates in creating resources and documentation. Tutorials, guides, and documentation repositories help newcomers and experienced developers alike. These resources contribute to the accessibility and learning curve of graphics programming.

### **4. Organizing Events and Conferences**

Graphics-focused events and conferences bring the community together in person. Events like SIGGRAPH provide a platform **for** researchers and practitioners to showcase their work, exchange ideas, and inspire others. Such gatherings foster networking and collaboration.

```markdown

```plaintext

Join us at WebGLCon 2023 **for** a two-day conference featuring talks and workshops on WebGL development.

### **5. Feedback and Improvement**

The community serves as a valuable source of feedback **for** graphics technologies. Developers can gather insights and user experiences to improve their projects. Feedback loops help identify bugs, performance issues, and usability concerns.

*### **6. Mentorship and Learning Opportunities***

Experienced developers often take on mentorship roles within the community. They guide newcomers, answer questions, and provide valuable insights. Mentorship programs and initiatives encourage skill development and knowledge transfer.

```markdown

```plaintext

Looking **for** a WebGL mentor? Our community offers mentorship programs **for** aspiring developers.

*### **7. Advocacy and Growth***

The graphics development community advocates **for** the adoption **and** growth of WebGL **and** OpenGL. Members promote the use of these technologies **in** various industries, **from** gaming **and** entertainment to data visualization **and** education.

*### **8. Challenges and Collaborative Problem Solving***

The community thrives on solving complex challenges collaboratively. When faced **with** difficult problems, developers often turn to the community **for** assistance. Collectively, they brainstorm solutions **and** share insights.

In summary, the community **is** a driving force behind the advancement of graphics development. Its role **in** sharing knowledge, fostering open source collaboration, creating resources,

**and** advocating **for** WebGL **and** OpenGL ensures the continued growth **and** innovation **in** the field. Developers, whether experienced **or** newcomers, can benefit **from** active participation **in** the graphics development community.

---

## Section 18.2: Contributing to OpenGL and WebGL Open Source Projects

Contributing to open source projects related to OpenGL and WebGL is a rewarding way to engage with the graphics development community. This section explores the steps and best practices for actively participating in these projects, whether you're a developer looking to give back or a newcomer eager to get involved.

### 1. Choosing a Project

Start by identifying open source projects that align with your interests and expertise. Many libraries and tools are available, covering a wide range of topics, from rendering engines to utilities for shader development. Popular projects include Three.js, Babylon.js, and GLFW.

### 2. Exploring Documentation and Issue Tracker

Before diving into code contributions, familiarize yourself with the project's documentation and issue tracker. Understanding the project's goals, guidelines, and existing issues will help you get started on the right foot.

### 3. Forking the Repository

To contribute to an open source project, begin by forking its repository on platforms like GitHub. This creates a copy of the project under your account, allowing you to work on changes independently.

## 4. Cloning the Repository

Once you've forked the repository, clone it to your local development environment. This step enables you to make changes and test them before submitting them back to the main project.

```*shell*

git clone https://github.com/yourusername/projectname.git

5. Branching and Development

Create a new branch for your work. It's essential to keep your changes isolated from the main project's codebase. This practice simplifies collaboration and ensures that your contributions don't interfere with ongoing development.

```markdown

```shell

git checkout -b feature-name

*### **6. Making Code Changes***

Now, you can make code changes that align with your contribution goals. Follow the project's coding standards and guidelines, and document your changes clearly. Be mindful of the project's scope and maintain backward compatibility **when** necessary.

*### **7. Testing and Quality Assurance***
```

Thoroughly test your code changes to ensure they work as intended. Write unit tests and conduct manual testing where applicable. Address any issues or bugs that you encounter during testing.

*### **8. Committing and Pushing***

Commit your changes to your branch and push them to your forked repository. Make your commit messages descriptive and concise, explaining the purpose of **each** change.

```markdown

```shell

git commit -m "Added feature X"

git push origin feature-name

### **9. Creating a Pull Request**

Once your changes are committed and pushed, initiate a pull request (PR) to the main project's repository. Provide a clear description of your changes, including their purpose and any relevant context.

### **10. Review and Collaboration**

Be open to feedback and collaboration. Maintainers and other contributors may review your PR, suggest improvements, or request changes. Engage in constructive discussions to address feedback and make necessary adjustments.

### **11. Continuous Integration**

Many open source projects use continuous integration (CI) tools to automatically test and verify code changes. Ensure that your contributions pass these tests to maintain the project's integrity.

### **12. Documentation and Comments**

In addition to code, consider contributing to documentation. Clear and comprehensive documentation is invaluable for users and fellow developers. You can also help by answering questions and providing assistance in the project's community channels.

### **13. Recognition and Community Building**

Contributing to open source projects is a chance to showcase your skills and build your reputation in the community. It's also an opportunity to connect with like-minded individuals who share your passion for graphics programming.

In conclusion, contributing to open source projects related to OpenGL and WebGL is an excellent way to give back to the community, improve your skills, and collaborate with fellow developers. By following best practices and actively participating in the project's development process, you can make a meaningful impact and be a valuable member of the graphics development community.

## Section 18.3: Leveraging Community Knowledge and Resources

Engaging with the OpenGL and WebGL communities provides valuable opportunities for knowledge sharing and resource access. In this section, we explore how you can tap into these communities to enhance your graphics programming skills and stay updated with the latest developments.

## 1. Online Forums and Discussion Boards

Joining online forums and discussion boards is an effective way to connect with fellow graphics developers. Platforms like Stack Overflow, Reddit's r/GraphicsProgramming, and dedicated OpenGL and WebGL forums host discussions, share insights, and provide solutions to common challenges. Actively participate by asking questions and contributing answers to build your reputation within the community.

## 2. Social Media and Networking

Follow graphics programming experts, projects, and organizations on social media platforms like Twitter and LinkedIn. These platforms often share tutorials, articles, and news related to OpenGL and WebGL. Additionally, consider participating in graphics-related groups or communities to network with professionals in the field.

## 3. GitHub and Source Code Repositories

GitHub is a hub for open source graphics projects. Explore repositories, follow projects that interest you, and star those you find useful. This will help you keep track of updates and discover new libraries, tools, and resources.

## 4. Online Courses and Tutorials

Numerous online courses and tutorials are available for learning OpenGL and WebGL. Websites like Udemy, Coursera, and Khan Academy offer courses covering various aspects of graphics programming. These resources often include video lectures, coding exercises, and assignments to reinforce your learning.

## 5. Graphics Conferences and Meetups

Graphics conferences and meetups provide opportunities to learn from experts, attend workshops, and connect with professionals in the field. Conferences like SIGGRAPH and WebGL Meetups offer valuable insights, presentations, and networking opportunities.

## 6. Reading Books and Documentation

Books dedicated to OpenGL and WebGL, as well as official documentation, are invaluable resources for in-depth learning. Reading books written by experts in the field can provide comprehensive knowledge and insights into graphics programming.

## 7. Online Courses and Tutorials

Numerous online courses and tutorials are available for learning OpenGL and WebGL. Websites like Udemy, Coursera, and Khan Academy offer courses covering various aspects of graphics programming. These resources often include video lectures, coding exercises, and assignments to reinforce your learning.

## 8. Graphics Conferences and Meetups

Graphics conferences and meetups provide opportunities to learn from experts, attend workshops, and connect with professionals in the field. Conferences like SIGGRAPH and WebGL Meetups offer valuable insights, presentations, and networking opportunities.

## 9. Reading Books and Documentation

Books dedicated to OpenGL and WebGL, as well as official documentation, are invaluable resources for in-depth learning. Reading books written by experts in the field can provide comprehensive knowledge and insights into graphics programming.

### 10. Collaboration and Contributions

Consider collaborating with peers on graphics projects. This can be a great way to learn from others, share your expertise, and collectively tackle challenging problems. Open source projects related to graphics programming often welcome contributions, providing a platform for learning through practical involvement.

### 11. Stay Informed

Graphics programming is a rapidly evolving field. Stay informed about the latest trends, updates, and advancements by following blogs, news websites, and community announcements. Subscribe to newsletters and mailing lists to receive regular updates on graphics-related topics.

In summary, leveraging the knowledge and resources available within the OpenGL and WebGL communities is essential for your growth as a graphics programmer. By actively participating in discussions, networking with peers, accessing tutorials, and staying updated with the latest developments, you can enhance your skills and contribute meaningfully to the field of graphics programming.

## Section 18.4: Case Studies: Successful Community Projects

In this section, we'll explore a few case studies of successful community projects in the world of OpenGL and WebGL graphics programming. These projects demonstrate the power of collaboration and open source development in advancing the field.

## 1. Three.js: A Popular WebGL Framework

Three.js is a JavaScript library that simplifies 3D graphics programming with WebGL. It offers a wide range of features for creating 3D scenes, handling animations, and working with textures and materials. Three.js is widely used in the WebGL community and has a thriving developer community.

Three.js demonstrates the impact of open source collaboration. It has a large number of contributors who have collectively improved the library's features, performance, and documentation. The community actively shares knowledge through forums and repositories, making it easier for developers to create stunning 3D web applications.

## 2. GLM: The OpenGL Mathematics Library

GLM is a header-only C++ mathematics library designed for graphics programming with OpenGL. It provides vector and matrix operations, quaternions, and geometry utilities commonly used in graphics applications. GLM's simplicity, efficiency, and compatibility with OpenGL make it a preferred choice for many developers.

GLM's success can be attributed to its open source nature. Developers from various backgrounds have contributed to the library's development, enhancing its functionality and performance. GLM is widely adopted in the graphics community, emphasizing the importance of accessible and collaborative math libraries.

## 3. Blender: A 3D Content Creation Suite

Blender is an open source 3D computer graphics software used for modeling, animation, rendering, and more. It has a large and active user community, including artists, animators, and developers.

Blender's success as a comprehensive 3D suite is a testament to the power of community-driven development.

Blender's open source model has allowed artists and developers to collaborate closely. Users contribute to the software by creating plugins, sharing assets, and providing feedback. This community-driven approach has led to Blender's continuous improvement and its role as a major player in the 3D graphics industry.

## 4. GLEW: The OpenGL Extension Wrangler Library

GLEW is a C library that simplifies the management of OpenGL extensions across different platforms. It provides a straightforward way to access OpenGL extensions and functions, ensuring compatibility with various GPUs and drivers. GLEW's ease of use and effectiveness have made it a staple in the OpenGL community.

GLEW's success is a result of its open source development. The library has benefited from contributions by developers who have expanded its support for new extensions and platforms. GLEW demonstrates how collaborative efforts can streamline the process of working with complex graphics APIs like OpenGL.

## 5. Godot Engine: An Open Source Game Engine

Godot Engine is an open source game engine that supports both 2D and 3D game development. It features a user-friendly interface, a scripting language, and a dedicated community. Godot's growth and feature-rich environment are driven by its open source nature and active community participation.

Godot's community actively contributes to its development by creating plugins, templates, and game assets. Users also share their knowledge through tutorials and forums, making it easier for newcomers to learn and create games. The success of Godot highlights the impact of open source game engines in democratizing game development.

These case studies underscore the significance of community-driven projects in the world of OpenGL and WebGL graphics programming. The success of these projects results from the collaborative efforts of developers, artists, and enthusiasts who contribute their time, expertise, and creativity to advance the field and make powerful tools and libraries accessible to all.

## Section 18.5: Growing the Graphics Programming Community

In this final section of Chapter 18, we will discuss the importance of growing the graphics programming community. A vibrant and active community is essential for the advancement of graphics programming, as it fosters knowledge sharing, collaboration, and innovation.

### 1. Mentorship and Education

One of the most effective ways to grow the graphics programming community is through mentorship and education. Experienced developers can mentor newcomers, helping them learn the ropes, troubleshoot issues, and navigate the complexities of graphics programming. Online tutorials, courses, and workshops also play a crucial role in educating aspiring developers and expanding the community's knowledge base.

Mentoring and education programs can be organized by individuals, educational institutions, or organizations focused on graphics programming. These initiatives contribute to a continuous influx of new talent and fresh perspectives into the community.

## 2. Open Source Contributions

Encouraging open source contributions is another vital aspect of community growth. When developers and artists contribute to open source projects, they not only enhance their skills but also make valuable contributions to the wider community. Projects such as GitHub and GitLab have made it easier than ever to collaborate on open source graphics software, libraries, and tools.

Community leaders and project maintainers can facilitate open source contributions by providing clear guidelines, documentation, and issue tracking systems. They can also mentor new contributors and help them get started with the development process.

## 3. Collaboration and Networking

Graphics programming conferences, meetups, and online forums offer opportunities for professionals and enthusiasts to connect, collaborate, and share ideas. Attending conferences like SIGGRAPH and GDC can provide valuable insights and foster networking within the industry.

Online forums and communities, such as Stack Overflow, Reddit, and specialized graphics programming forums, serve as platforms for asking questions, sharing knowledge, and discussing industry trends. These platforms facilitate discussions, problem-solving, and the exchange of best practices among community members.

## 4. Diversity and Inclusion

Ensuring diversity and inclusion within the graphics programming community is crucial for its growth and innovation. A diverse community brings together individuals with different backgrounds, experiences, and perspectives, leading to a richer pool of ideas and solutions.

Community leaders and organizations can take proactive steps to promote diversity and inclusion, such as creating safe and welcoming environments, offering scholarships or grants, and actively seeking contributions from underrepresented groups.

## 5. Outreach and Education Programs

Outreach and education programs that target students and newcomers to the field can play a significant role in expanding the graphics programming community. These programs can include coding bootcamps, workshops, and outreach to schools and colleges to introduce students to graphics programming concepts.

By investing in outreach and education, the community can inspire the next generation of graphics programmers and ensure a sustainable pipeline of talent.

## 6. Supporting Emerging Technologies

Graphics programming is a field that constantly evolves, driven by advances in hardware and software technologies. To stay relevant, the community must embrace emerging technologies such as real-time ray tracing, machine learning for graphics, and augmented reality.

Supporting and exploring these emerging technologies not only keeps the community at the forefront of innovation but also attracts developers and researchers who are excited about pushing the boundaries of graphics programming.

In conclusion, growing the graphics programming community requires a concerted effort from both individuals and organizations.

By fostering mentorship, encouraging open source contributions, facilitating collaboration and networking, promoting diversity and inclusion, investing in outreach and education, and embracing emerging technologies, the community can continue to thrive and push the boundaries of what is possible in graphics programming. As the field continues to evolve, a strong and vibrant community will play a pivotal role in shaping its future.

# Chapter 19: The Future of WebGL and OpenGL

## Section 19.1: Current Trends in Graphics Programming

In this section, we will explore the current trends in graphics programming, focusing on both WebGL and OpenGL. Understanding these trends is essential for developers and enthusiasts who want to stay up-to-date with the rapidly evolving field of graphics programming.

### 1. Real-Time Ray Tracing

One of the most significant trends in graphics programming is the adoption of real-time ray tracing. This technique, long reserved for offline rendering due to its computational intensity, is now becoming feasible for real-time applications. Graphics APIs like DirectX 12 Ultimate and NVIDIA's RTX platform have made real-time ray tracing more accessible, allowing developers to achieve photorealistic lighting and reflections in games and simulations.

### 2. Machine Learning Integration

Machine learning is increasingly being integrated into graphics programming. AI-powered techniques are used for tasks like upscaling lower-resolution textures, denoising rendered images, and even generating content. NVIDIA's DLSS (Deep Learning Super Sampling) is a prime example, using AI to upscale lower-resolution images to higher-quality results in real-time.

## 3. Virtual and Augmented Reality

The fields of virtual reality (VR) and augmented reality (AR) continue to grow, with WebGL and OpenGL playing vital roles in their development. VR offers immersive experiences, while AR enhances the real world with digital elements. These technologies have applications in gaming, education, healthcare, and more.

## 4. Web-Based Graphics

WebGL remains a key technology for web-based graphics. With advancements in browser capabilities and hardware acceleration, web developers can create sophisticated 3D and VR experiences directly in the browser. This trend empowers web designers to incorporate interactive 3D content into websites and web applications.

## 5. Cross-Platform Development

Developers increasingly seek tools and frameworks that enable cross-platform development between desktop and mobile platforms. This trend simplifies the process of creating applications that can run seamlessly on various devices, including PCs, smartphones, and tablets.

## 6. Shader Languages and HLSL

Shader languages like GLSL (OpenGL Shading Language) and HLSL (High-Level Shading Language) continue to evolve. These languages are essential for graphics programming, as they enable developers to create custom shaders for rendering effects. Staying updated with the latest shader language features and optimizations is crucial for achieving cutting-edge graphics.

## 7. Performance Optimization

As hardware capabilities grow, optimizing graphics applications for performance remains a constant concern. Efficient rendering, reduced latency, and minimal resource consumption are priorities for developers. Tools for profiling and debugging graphics code are essential for achieving optimal performance.

## 8. WebGL in Web Development

WebGL is increasingly used in web development beyond graphics and gaming. It enables data visualization, scientific simulations, and interactive educational content directly in web browsers. This trend expands the range of applications that leverage WebGL's capabilities.

## 9. Graphics APIs

Graphics APIs like Vulkan, DirectX 12, and Metal continue to compete and innovate. Developers should stay informed about the capabilities and advantages of these APIs to choose the best fit for their projects, depending on the target platforms and requirements.

## 10. Open Source Communities

Open source projects related to graphics programming are thriving. These communities offer valuable resources, libraries, and tools that simplify development and foster collaboration. Contributing to and leveraging open source projects is a growing trend in the graphics programming ecosystem.

In conclusion, the field of graphics programming is dynamic and constantly evolving. Staying informed about these trends and adopting new technologies and techniques is essential for developers and enthusiasts who want to remain at the forefront of this exciting and innovative field. As WebGL and OpenGL continue to adapt to new hardware and software advancements, they will play integral roles in shaping the future of graphics programming.

## Section 19.2: Emerging Technologies in WebGL and OpenGL

In this section, we will explore emerging technologies and trends in WebGL and OpenGL. These technologies represent the future of graphics programming and have the potential to transform the way we create and interact with digital visual content.

### 1. WebGPU: The Next-Generation Graphics API

WebGPU is an emerging standard that aims to provide a modern, low-level graphics and compute API for the web. It's designed to be more efficient and flexible than WebGL and offers better integration with modern hardware. WebGPU will enable developers to harness the full power of GPUs, allowing for more advanced graphics and compute workloads on the web.

### 2. Vulkan for the Web

Vulkan is a high-performance, cross-platform graphics API that has gained popularity in desktop and mobile development. Efforts are underway to bring Vulkan support to the web, enabling web developers to take advantage of its performance benefits. This could lead to more sophisticated web-based 3D applications and games.

### 3. WebAssembly (Wasm) Enhancements

WebAssembly (Wasm) is a binary instruction format for web browsers that enables near-native performance for web applications. It's becoming increasingly important for graphics programming in the browser. Emerging enhancements in Wasm, such as multi-threading support, will allow for more efficient and parallel execution of graphics code, further improving performance.

## 4. Real-Time Collaboration in 3D Environments

Collaboration in 3D environments is gaining traction. WebGL and OpenGL are being used to create shared virtual spaces where multiple users can interact and collaborate in real time. These environments find applications in remote work, education, and virtual events.

## 5. AI-Driven Content Generation

Artificial intelligence is being used to generate graphics content, including textures, models, and animations. Machine learning models can create realistic environments and characters, reducing the manual effort required for asset creation in games and simulations.

## 6. Augmented Reality (AR) for the Web

Web-based AR experiences are on the rise, thanks to WebGL and emerging web standards. AR applications on the web enable users to interact with digital objects in the real world through their web browsers. This trend has implications for e-commerce, education, and entertainment.

## 7. 3D Web Design Tools

Web-based 3D design tools are becoming more accessible. These tools, often powered by WebGL, enable designers and artists to create 3D content directly in their browsers. They can be used for product design, architectural visualization, and creative art projects.

## 8. Continued VR/AR Integration

The integration of virtual reality (VR) and augmented reality (AR) with WebGL and OpenGL is an ongoing trend. As VR and AR hardware becomes more widespread, developers will continue to explore innovative ways to blend digital and physical worlds.

## 9. Cross-Platform Deployment

Efforts to streamline cross-platform deployment of WebGL and OpenGL applications are ongoing. Developers are looking for ways to create content that can run seamlessly on various platforms, including desktop, mobile, and web, without major code changes.

## 10. WebXR: Expanding Immersive Experiences

WebXR is an API that enables immersive experiences on the web, including VR and AR. It allows developers to build web-based XR applications that work across different devices and browsers. The continued development of WebXR will make it easier for developers to create immersive content for a broader audience.

In conclusion, WebGL and OpenGL are at the forefront of emerging technologies in graphics programming. As these technologies continue to evolve, they will enable more immersive, efficient, and accessible graphics experiences on the web and across various platforms. Developers who embrace these trends and stay updated with the latest developments will be well-positioned to shape the future of graphics programming.

# Section 19.3: The Future of Integrated Graphics Environments

In this section, we will delve into the future of integrated graphics environments, exploring the possibilities and directions in which WebGL and OpenGL are heading. The rapidly evolving landscape of graphics programming promises exciting developments that will shape the way we interact with digital visuals.

## 1. Unified Graphics Ecosystem

One of the key directions for WebGL and OpenGL is the development of a more unified graphics ecosystem. Efforts are being made to bridge the gap between different graphics standards and APIs, making it easier for developers to create content that seamlessly works across various platforms, including desktop, mobile, and the web.

## 2. Improved Realism and Immersion

The pursuit of realism and immersion in graphics programming continues. Advanced rendering techniques, physically-based rendering, and more sophisticated shaders will lead to visually stunning graphics that approach photorealism. This trend is particularly relevant for gaming, simulations, and virtual environments.

## 3. Enhanced Performance and Optimization

Performance optimization remains a priority. Future iterations of WebGL and OpenGL will introduce features and tools to further optimize graphics applications. This includes better utilization of multi-core processors, improved memory management, and enhanced rendering pipelines to achieve smoother, more responsive experiences.

## 4. Ray Tracing Integration

Ray tracing, a technique that simulates the behavior of light in a scene, is making its way into real-time graphics. While traditionally associated with offline rendering, advancements in hardware and software will enable more widespread use of ray tracing in WebGL and OpenGL applications. This will result in more realistic lighting, reflections, and shadows.

## 5. Cross-Device and Cross-Reality Experiences

The future of integrated graphics environments will be about providing consistent experiences across a range of devices, from traditional screens to augmented reality (AR) and virtual reality (VR) headsets. Seamless transitions between these modes will allow users to interact with content in the most suitable way for their context.

## 6. Web3D and the Metaverse

The concept of the metaverse, a collective virtual shared space, is gaining momentum. WebGL and OpenGL will play a crucial role in building the 3D web infrastructure required for the metaverse. This includes creating interconnected virtual worlds, social experiences, and immersive online environments.

## 7. Machine Learning and Procedural Content

Machine learning algorithms will increasingly be used to generate and enhance graphics content. This includes the automatic generation of textures, 3D models, and animations. Procedural content generation, driven by AI, will reduce the manual labor involved in asset creation for games and simulations.

## 8. WebGPU Adoption

As WebGPU matures, it will likely become the de facto standard for web-based graphics programming. Its lower-level, multi-threaded approach will enable developers to harness the full power of modern GPUs, resulting in more performant and visually impressive web applications.

## 9. Accessibility and Inclusivity

Future graphics environments will place a strong emphasis on accessibility and inclusivity. This means ensuring that 3D and VR/ AR experiences are usable by individuals with disabilities. Advances in user interfaces, haptic feedback, and assistive technologies will contribute to a more inclusive digital world.

## 10. Sustainability and Efficiency

The environmental impact of graphics rendering is a growing concern. Future developments will focus on optimizing power consumption and resource utilization, ensuring that graphics applications are more energy-efficient and sustainable.

In conclusion, the future of integrated graphics environments in WebGL and OpenGL is marked by exciting advancements in realism, performance, and accessibility. These technologies will continue to enable the creation of immersive experiences across a wide range of devices and platforms, paving the way for the next generation of interactive digital content. Developers who embrace these trends will be at the forefront of shaping this future landscape.

## Section 19.4: Predictions and Speculations

In this section, we'll explore some predictions and speculations about the future of WebGL and OpenGL. While we can't predict the future with certainty, we can identify trends and emerging technologies that are likely to have an impact on the graphics programming landscape.

### 1. Convergence of WebGL and OpenGL

One prediction is that the gap between WebGL and OpenGL will continue to narrow. As web technologies evolve and become more capable, WebGL will likely incorporate features from OpenGL, and vice versa. This convergence will simplify the development process, allowing developers to use a more consistent set of tools and APIs across web and desktop environments.

### 2. WebAssembly and Native Performance

With the continued development of WebAssembly (Wasm), which allows running native code in web browsers at near-native speeds, we can expect WebGL applications to benefit from improved performance. This may lead to more complex and computationally intensive graphics applications on the web.

```
// Example of using WebAssembly in WebGL

const module = new WebAssembly.Module(/* wasm binary data */);

const instance = new WebAssembly.Instance(module);

const exports = instance.exports;

// Use exports in WebGL application
```

3. Integration with WebXR

As augmented reality (AR) and virtual reality (VR) become more prevalent, WebGL and OpenGL are likely to integrate more closely with the WebXR standard. This integration will enable developers to build immersive AR and VR experiences directly within web browsers.

4. Continued Emphasis on Security

As graphics applications become more complex and interconnected, security will remain a top priority. WebGL and OpenGL will continue to evolve to address potential security vulnerabilities and ensure safe execution of graphics content in browsers.

```
// WebGL security best practice

gl.getExtension('WEBGL_lose_context').loseContext();
```

5. AI-Driven Graphics

Artificial intelligence (AI) and machine learning (ML) will play an increasing role in graphics programming. AI algorithms may assist in content generation, adaptive rendering, and even real-time procedural world-building for games and simulations.

```
# Example of using AI for image upscaling in WebGL

import tensorflow as tf

# Load a pre-trained AI model

model = tf.keras.models.load_model('super_resolution_model.h5')

# Use AI to upscale textures or images in WebGL
```

6. Environmental Considerations

Environmental concerns will influence the development of graphics technologies. Expect to see more focus on energy-efficient rendering techniques, reducing the carbon footprint of graphics-intensive applications.

```
// WebGL function for energy-efficient rendering

gl.enable(gl.ENERGY_SAVING_MODE);
```

7. Cross-Platform Accessibility

Efforts will continue to make WebGL and OpenGL content accessible to a broader audience, including individuals with disabilities. This may involve improved support for screen readers, voice commands, and haptic feedback.

```
<!—HTML5 ARIA attributes for WebGL accessibility—>

<canvas

id="glCanvas"

aria-label="Interactive 3D visualization"

role="application"

></canvas>
```

8. Quantum Computing Impact

The emergence of quantum computing could have profound implications for graphics programming. Quantum algorithms may accelerate tasks like ray tracing and physics simulations, opening up new possibilities for realistic graphics.

```
# Hypothetical quantum ray tracing function

def quantum_ray_trace(scene):

# Perform quantum ray tracing calculations

...

# Integrate quantum computing into WebGL/OpenGL pipelines
```

9. Decentralized Graphics and NFTs

The use of blockchain technology and non-fungible tokens (NFTs) for digital art and collectibles could lead to decentralized graphics applications. Artists and developers may explore new ways to create, distribute, and interact with digital graphics content.

10. Ethical Considerations

Ethical considerations, such as content moderation and privacy, will continue to be important in the graphics programming space. Developers and organizations will need to address these issues responsibly and transparently.

In summary, the future of WebGL and OpenGL holds exciting possibilities, driven by technological advancements, convergence of standards, and the evolving landscape of web and graphics technologies. While these predictions provide a glimpse into what may come, it's essential for developers to stay informed and adapt to the evolving graphics programming ecosystem.

Section 19.5: Preparing for Future Developments in Graphics Programming

As we look toward the future of graphics programming, it's essential for developers to prepare themselves for the evolving landscape. Here are some key strategies and considerations to help you stay ahead in the world of WebGL and OpenGL:

1. Lifelong Learning

Continual learning is fundamental in any field, and graphics programming is no exception. Stay updated with the latest developments, read research papers, and explore emerging technologies. Online courses, tutorials, and conferences are valuable resources for expanding your knowledge.

```
// Commit to lifelong learning

const learning = true;

while (learning) {

keepLearning();

}
```

2. Embrace Cross-Disciplinary Skills

Graphics programming often intersects with various domains, including mathematics, physics, and computer science. Having a strong foundation in these areas can be a significant advantage. Consider learning related disciplines to broaden your skill set.

```
# Embrace cross-disciplinary skills

import mathematics
```

```
import physics

import computer_science

# Apply interdisciplinary knowledge to graphics
```

3. Stay Agile and Adaptable

The technology landscape evolves rapidly. Be prepared to adapt to new tools, libraries, and paradigms. Familiarize yourself with multiple programming languages, as they may have applications beyond your current projects.

```
// Stay agile and adaptable

const technology = 'constantly evolving';

if (technology === 'constantly evolving') {

beAdaptable();

}
```

4. Collaborate and Network

Collaboration with peers and participation in the graphics programming community can lead to valuable insights and opportunities. Join forums, attend meetups, and contribute to open source projects. Networking can open doors to exciting projects and collaborations.

```
// Collaborate and network

const community = 'graphics_programmers';

if (community.includes('collaboration')) {

joinCommunity();
```

```
}
```

5. Explore Emerging Fields

Graphics programming is not limited to traditional graphics. Explore emerging fields such as data visualization, scientific simulations, and machine learning-driven graphics. These areas offer unique challenges and opportunities.

```
# Explore emerging fields

if 'data_visualization' in emerging_fields:

exploreDataViz()
```

6. Develop a Portfolio

Building a portfolio of your work is essential for showcasing your skills to potential employers or collaborators. Include a variety of projects that demonstrate your expertise in graphics programming.

```
// Develop a portfolio

const portfolio = [project1, project2, project3];

const impressEmployers = () => {

showPortfolio(portfolio);

};
```

7. Ethics and Responsibility

With great power comes great responsibility. Be mindful of the ethical implications of your work, especially in areas like AI-generated content and data privacy. Prioritize ethical considerations in your projects.

```
// Prioritize ethics and responsibility

const responsible = true;

if (responsible) {

considerEthicalImplications();

}
```

8. Keep an Eye on Hardware

Graphics programming is intimately tied to hardware capabilities. Stay informed about advancements in GPUs, CPUs, and specialized hardware like ray tracing cards. This knowledge can influence your approach to optimization and rendering techniques.

```
# Keep an eye on hardware advancements

if 'new_gpu' in hardware_advancements:

optimizeForNewHardware()
```

9. Mentorship and Education

Consider mentoring aspiring graphics programmers or sharing your knowledge through teaching. Mentorship not only benefits others but also reinforces your own understanding of the subject matter.

```
// Engage in mentorship and education

const mentorship = true;

if (mentorship) {

mentorStudents();

}
```

10. Stay Passionate

Finally, passion is the driving force behind innovation. Stay passionate about graphics programming, and let your enthusiasm fuel your creativity and problem-solving skills.

```
# Stay passionate about graphics programming

passion = True

while passion:

keepCreating()
```

In conclusion, the future of graphics programming promises exciting developments, but it also demands continuous growth and adaptability from professionals in the field. By following these strategies and embracing the evolving landscape, you can position yourself for success in the dynamic world of WebGL and OpenGL.

Chapter 20: Conclusion and Next Steps

Section 20.1: Summarizing Key Learnings

In this final chapter, we'll summarize the key learnings from this book, reflect on the best practices in WebGL and OpenGL, discuss potential future pathways in graphics programming, provide resources for continued learning, and offer some final thoughts and encouragement for aspiring developers.

Key Learnings

Throughout this book, we've covered a wide range of topics related to graphics programming. Some of the key takeaways include:

- Understanding the evolution of graphics programming, from early techniques to modern WebGL and OpenGL.

- Grasping the core concepts of OpenGL and WebGL, including their architectures and rendering pipelines.

- Learning how to set up environments for OpenGL and WebGL development.

- Exploring basic and advanced programming techniques for both platforms.

- Gaining insights into the graphics pipeline and optimizing graphics performance.

- Mastering shaders, which play a central role in modern graphics.

• Implementing textures, lighting models, and realistic shadows for immersive graphics.

• Working with 3D models, transformations, user interactions, and animations.

• Optimizing graphics applications for performance and debugging them effectively.

• Understanding the need for integration between OpenGL and WebGL and the challenges it presents.

• Exploring the role of WebGL in modern web development, including its integration with HTML, CSS, JavaScript, and web frameworks.

• Diving into advanced rendering techniques and their comparative analysis.

• Adapting graphics for mobile devices and exploring touch interactions.

• Implementing virtual and augmented reality in both OpenGL and WebGL.

• Learning porting strategies from desktop to browser environments.

• Addressing security and privacy concerns in web-based graphics.

• Exploring scalability, maintenance, and version control for graphics projects.

• Understanding the importance of community and open-source contributions.

• Examining current trends and emerging technologies in graphics programming.

• Preparing for the future of WebGL and OpenGL, considering interdisciplinary skills and ethical responsibilities.

Best Practices in WebGL and OpenGL

As you continue your journey in graphics programming, remember these best practices:

1. **Keep Learning:** Graphics programming is constantly evolving. Stay updated with new technologies, tools, and techniques.
2. **Master Shaders:** Shaders are at the heart of modern graphics. Invest time in understanding and optimizing them.
3. **Optimize for Performance:** Performance is crucial. Learn to optimize your code and leverage hardware capabilities.
4. **Collaborate and Network:** Join the graphics programming community, collaborate with peers, and contribute to open-source projects.
5. **Explore Diverse Fields:** Graphics programming extends beyond graphics. Explore fields like data visualization, simulations, and AI-driven graphics.
6. **Prioritize Ethics:** Be mindful of the ethical implications of your work, especially in areas like AI-generated content and data privacy.
7. **Stay Passionate:** Passion fuels creativity and innovation.

Stay enthusiastic about graphics programming.

Future Pathways in Graphics Programming

The future of WebGL and OpenGL holds exciting possibilities. Emerging technologies like real-time ray tracing, machine learning-driven graphics, and AR/VR integration are transforming the field. As a graphics programmer, you can explore these domains, contribute to their development, and shape the future of graphics.

Resources for Continued Learning

To continue your graphics programming journey, here are some valuable resources:

- Online courses and tutorials on graphics programming.
- Books and research papers in the field.
- Graphics programming forums and communities.
- Open-source graphics projects for hands-on experience.
- Conferences and meetups for networking and learning from experts.

Final Thoughts and Encouragement

Graphics programming is a dynamic and rewarding field that combines art and science. It offers opportunities to create visually stunning experiences, explore cutting-edge technologies, and push the boundaries of what's possible on computers and the web. As you embark on your graphics programming journey, remember that persistence, curiosity, and a passion for learning will be your greatest assets. Embrace challenges as opportunities for growth, and continue to create the graphics of the future.

Congratulations on completing this book, and best of luck with your graphics programming endeavors!

Section 20.2: Best Practices in WebGL and OpenGL

As you conclude your journey through this book, it's essential to recap some best practices in WebGL and OpenGL. These practices will not only help you in your current projects but also guide you in your future endeavors in the field of graphics programming.

1. Continuous Learning

Graphics programming is a rapidly evolving field. To stay relevant, make continuous learning a habit. Follow blogs, forums, and research papers related to WebGL and OpenGL. Attend conferences, workshops, and online courses to keep up with the latest developments.

2. Master Shaders

Shaders are the heart of modern graphics rendering. Spend time mastering shader programming in both OpenGL and WebGL. Understand vertex shaders, fragment shaders, and geometry shaders thoroughly. Optimize shaders for performance, and explore advanced shader techniques like tessellation and compute shaders.

```
// Example vertex shader in GLSL

#version 330 core

layout(location = 0) in vec3 inPosition;

uniform mat4 modelViewProjectionMatrix;
```

```
void main() {
gl_Position = modelViewProjectionMatrix * vec4(inPosition, 1.0);
}
```

3. Performance Optimization

Graphics performance can make or break user experiences. Learn to profile your code and use GPU debugging tools. Optimize your rendering pipeline by minimizing redundant calculations and reducing the number of draw calls. Employ techniques like frustum culling and level-of-detail (LOD) to improve performance in complex scenes.

4. Collaboration and Networking

Join the graphics programming community. Collaborate with peers, participate in open-source projects, and share your knowledge. Online forums and social media platforms dedicated to graphics programming are excellent places to connect with like-minded individuals.

5. Diversify Your Skills

While WebGL and OpenGL are your primary focus, consider diversifying your skills. Graphics programming can intersect with other fields like data visualization, scientific simulations, and artificial intelligence. Expanding your expertise beyond graphics can open up new opportunities.

6. Ethical Considerations

As graphics programmers, it's essential to consider the ethical implications of your work. This is especially relevant in areas like

AI-generated content and data privacy. Be mindful of how your creations impact society and individuals.

7. Stay Passionate

Graphics programming is an art as much as it is a science. Passion drives creativity and innovation. Stay enthusiastic about what you do, and let your love for graphics programming shine through in your projects.

In summary, WebGL and OpenGL offer incredible opportunities for creating visually stunning and interactive experiences. By following these best practices and staying committed to your learning journey, you can become a proficient graphics programmer and contribute to the ever-evolving world of computer graphics.

Section 20.3: Future Pathways in Graphics Programming

As you wrap up your exploration of WebGL and OpenGL, it's essential to consider the future pathways in graphics programming. This field is dynamic and constantly evolving, driven by advancements in technology, new hardware capabilities, and emerging trends. Here, we'll discuss some exciting directions that graphics programming is likely to take in the coming years.

1. Real-Time Ray Tracing

Ray tracing has long been hailed as the holy grail of rendering due to its ability to simulate the behavior of light realistically. While traditionally computationally expensive, recent advancements in hardware, such as dedicated ray tracing cores in GPUs, have made real-time ray tracing a reality. Expect to see more games and applications leveraging ray tracing for stunning visuals.

```
// Pseudocode for a simple ray tracing shader
RayTraceResult TraceRay(Ray ray, Scene scene) {
if (Intersects(ray, scene)) {
// Handle reflections, refractions, and material properties
// ...
return ComputeColor(ray, scene);
} else {
return SkyboxColor(ray);
}
}
```

2. Machine Learning and Graphics

Machine learning (ML) is making its mark in graphics programming. ML techniques are used for tasks like denoising, upscaling, and procedural content generation. With the integration of neural networks and graphics pipelines, we can expect more AI-driven graphics applications, including character animation and image synthesis.

```
# Example of using ML for denoising in image rendering
import tensorflow as tf
# Define and train a denoising neural network
denoiser = tf.keras.models.Sequential([...])
denoiser.compile([...])
```

```
denoiser.fit([...])

# Apply denoising during rendering

noisy_image = RenderScene(scene)

denoised_image = denoiser(noisy_image)
```

3. WebGL and WebXR Integration

WebGL's role in web development will continue to expand. Integration with WebXR (Web Extended Reality) will enable web-based augmented and virtual reality experiences directly in your browser. This will lead to innovative applications in gaming, education, and immersive storytelling.

```
// Example of WebGL and WebXR integration for VR experience

const xrSession = navigator.xr.requestSession('immersive-vr');

const gl = canvas.getContext('webgl');

xrSession.updateRenderState({

baseLayer: new XRWebGLLayer(xrSession, gl)

});

xrSession.requestAnimationFrame(drawScene);
```

4. Global Illumination

Achieving realistic global illumination in real-time graphics has been a long-standing challenge. Advances in algorithms and hardware will bring us closer to achieving this goal. Graphics programmers will work on solutions for simulating indirect lighting, soft shadows, and intricate light bounces.

```
// Pseudocode for global illumination computation
for each pixel in the frame {
Ray ray = CreatePrimaryRay(pixel);
Color result = TraceRay(ray, scene, maxBounces);
AccumulateResult(pixel, result);
}
```

5. Cross-Platform Development

The demand for cross-platform applications will persist. Graphics programmers will continue to explore frameworks and tools that allow them to write code once and deploy it across multiple platforms, including desktop, mobile, and the web.

6. Ethics and Responsible AI

As AI plays a more significant role in graphics, ethical considerations become critical. Graphics programmers will need to address issues related to biased algorithms, deepfakes, and privacy concerns. Ethical AI development practices will be an essential aspect of the field.

In conclusion, the world of graphics programming is filled with opportunities and challenges. By staying informed, embracing emerging technologies, and considering ethical implications, you can navigate this dynamic field successfully. Whether you're creating breathtaking visuals, immersive experiences, or pushing the boundaries of real-time rendering, the future of graphics programming holds exciting possibilities.

Section 20.4: Resources for Continued Learning

As you reach the final section of this book, it's essential to consider your journey in graphics programming as an ongoing process. Technology evolves rapidly, and to stay at the forefront of this field, you'll need to continue learning and expanding your skills. Here, we'll provide you with valuable resources to aid your ongoing education in graphics programming.

1. Online Courses and Tutorials

The internet is a treasure trove of online courses and tutorials covering a wide range of graphics programming topics. Platforms like Coursera, edX, Udemy, and Khan Academy offer courses on OpenGL, WebGL, computer graphics, and related subjects. Many of these courses are created by renowned institutions and experts.

2. Books and Documentation

Books remain a timeless source of knowledge. To dive deeper into specific areas of graphics programming, consider reading books dedicated to OpenGL, WebGL, computer graphics algorithms, and real-time rendering techniques. Additionally, always refer to official documentation for the latest updates and specifications.

3. Community Forums and Blogs

Participating in graphics programming communities can be incredibly enriching. Websites like Stack Overflow, Reddit's r/GraphicsProgramming, and the OpenGL Community Forum are excellent places to seek help, share knowledge, and stay updated on industry trends. Many experienced programmers also maintain blogs where they share insights, tips, and code samples.

4. GitHub and Open Source Projects

GitHub hosts numerous open-source graphics projects. Exploring these projects, contributing to them, and studying their source code can provide valuable hands-on experience. You can also use GitHub to showcase your own graphics programming projects, collaborate with others, and receive feedback.

```
# Clone an open-source WebGL project

git clone https://github.com/user/webgl-game.git
```

5. YouTube and Video Tutorials

YouTube hosts countless video tutorials on graphics programming topics. Channels like "TheCherno" and "ThinMatrix" offer in-depth tutorials on OpenGL and game development. Videos can be a great way to grasp complex concepts through visual explanations.

6. Hackathons and Competitions

Participating in graphics-related hackathons and coding competitions can be both fun and educational. Competing against others and tackling real-world challenges can hone your skills and provide exposure to innovative ideas.

7. University Courses and Degrees

Consider enrolling in university courses or pursuing a degree in computer graphics, computer science, or a related field. Formal education can provide you with a strong foundation and access to expert guidance.

8. Professional Organizations and Conferences

Joining professional organizations like SIGGRAPH (Special Interest Group on Computer Graphics and Interactive Techniques) can connect you with fellow graphics professionals and grant access to conferences, workshops, and publications.

9. Industry Journals and Publications

Keep an eye on academic journals and publications related to computer graphics. They contain cutting-edge research, algorithms, and techniques that can inspire your work.

10. Networking and Collaboration

Building a network of fellow graphics programmers and industry professionals can lead to collaborations and career opportunities. Attend industry events, conferences, and meetups to connect with like-minded individuals.

In your journey as a graphics programmer, continuous learning is the key to staying relevant and achieving your goals. Whether you're a hobbyist, a student, or a professional, these resources will help you expand your knowledge and make meaningful contributions to the exciting world of graphics programming.

Section 20.5: Final Thoughts and Encouragement for Aspiring Developers

As we conclude this comprehensive journey through the world of graphics programming, it's important to reflect on your growth, acknowledge your achievements, and set the stage for your future endeavors in this field. Whether you are a seasoned graphics programmer or someone just starting, your commitment to mastering this complex discipline is commendable. Here are some final thoughts and words of encouragement to keep you motivated:

1. Celebrate Your Progress

Take a moment to appreciate how far you've come. Graphics programming can be challenging, and the fact that you've navigated through this book demonstrates your dedication and passion for the subject. Every line of code you've written and every concept you've grasped is a significant achievement.

2. Embrace Challenges

Graphics programming is a dynamic field that constantly evolves. Don't be discouraged by challenges; instead, embrace them as opportunities for growth. The problems you encounter and solve along the way will only make you a more proficient developer.

3. Keep Experimenting

The beauty of graphics programming lies in its creative potential. Don't limit yourself to following existing tutorials or examples. Explore new ideas, experiment with different techniques, and don't be afraid to create your own projects. Innovation often arises from pushing boundaries.

4. Stay Curious

Graphics programming is a vast domain with numerous subfields and specializations. Whether it's real-time rendering, virtual reality, or mobile graphics, there is always something new to learn. Cultivate a curious mindset, and never stop seeking knowledge.

5. Collaborate and Share

Collaboration with peers and sharing your knowledge can be immensely rewarding. Engage with the graphics programming community, contribute to open-source projects, and help others who are on their learning journey. Teaching can deepen your understanding of the subject.

```
// A function to inspire and motivate

void inspireAspiringDevelopers() {

cout << "You have the power to shape the virtual world and create stunning visuals." << endl;

cout << "Every line of code you write brings you closer to your artistic vision." << endl;

cout << "Graphics programming is an art, a science, and a journey of endless discovery." << endl;

cout << "Embrace the challenge, stay curious, and never stop creating." << endl;

cout << "You are the architect of digital dreams. Keep coding and keep dreaming!" << endl;

}
```

6. Set Goals and Keep Learning

Define your goals and aspirations within graphics programming. Whether you want to work in the gaming industry, create interactive web experiences, or explore cutting-edge VR/AR technologies, set clear objectives and work toward them methodically.

7. Adapt to Industry Trends

The graphics programming field is heavily influenced by industry trends and technological advancements. Stay updated with the latest developments and adapt your skills to meet the demands of the industry.

8. Maintain a Work-Life Balance

While it's important to be passionate about your work, remember to maintain a healthy work-life balance. Take breaks, pursue other interests, and spend time with loved ones. A well-balanced life can enhance your creativity and overall well-being.

In conclusion, your journey in graphics programming is a testament to your commitment to creativity and technology. Whether you choose to continue developing stunning visual experiences, contribute to groundbreaking research, or inspire the next generation of developers, your contribution to this field is invaluable. Graphics programming is an art form, a science, and an ever-evolving adventure. Keep coding, keep exploring, and keep pushing the boundaries of what's possible in the world of computer graphics. The digital canvas is yours to paint, and your imagination is the only limit.

Milton Keynes UK
Ingram Content Group UK Ltd.
UKHW010835071223
433828UK00001B/49

9 798223 496045